FADE TO GRAY

by Richard Masinton
With an introduction by Ruth Ingall

DORRANCE
PUBLISHING CO
EST. 1920
PITTSBURGH, PENNSYLVANIA 15238

Dorrance Publishing Co
585 Alpha Drive
Suite 103
Pittsburgh, PA 15238
Visit our website at www.dorrancebookstore.com

ISBN: 978-1-4809-8691-6
eISBN: 978-1-4809-9209-2

To Dana:

Surely some songs, images, and dreams live somewhere in her brain and every so often may surface to a conscious level. Hopefully they comfort her and will never disappear until her brain shuts down completely. God bless her.

Contents

Acknowledgments

Julia A. Files, MD: My doctor, my friend, and my guardian angel. She saved my life.

Dawn Vandeberg: The best daughter in the world. She unselfishly came to help every time I asked and many times when I didn't ask. Words are inadequate to describe her love for me and mine for her.

Chuck and Jennifer Laue: Our dearest friends and among the last people that faded from Dana's mind. Not enough good things can happen to them. Jennifer and Dana were a real estate selling machine.

Bill and Carolyn Patterson: Our wonderful, steadfast friends who were always there when needed. Their friendship was a source of my strength.

Gretchen Losurdo, RN: A world class relief pitcher and a superb nurse advocate. She struck out the side.

Carol Brown, Dorothy Osborne, and Michelle Monaco: Dana's dear friends, partners, and birthday buddies over thirty-five years of girlfriend shenanigans.

Richard Caselli, MD: He made the medical side of Alzheimer's understandable and bearable. A brilliant, gentle, and compassionate physician, he has a gift that few have.

All the doctors and staff at the Mayo Clinic, at the Mayo Clinic Hospital and Specialty Building, and particularly at Medallion: we can't thank you enough.

Michael Monaco, MD: Our doctor before Mayo Clinic and Dana's doctor since. His demeanor, his care, and his understanding continue to be comforting.

Dana's real estate colleagues at JC Nichols Real Estate: she loved you all.

Jerry Pullins: For understanding how to care for Alzheimer's victims. He gets it, and his staff at SeniorCare live it every day.

The board of directors and officers of the Federal Home Loan Bank of Topeka and their spouses and partners: for their understanding, patience, and help.

Boomer: My buddy, my pal. He never left my side.

And, most of all, my partner Ruth Ingall without whose inspiration, encouragement and support, this book would not have been written. She lifted me when I was down, soothed me when it was needed, and prodded me when it was warranted. This is Dana's story, and it is my book, both of which are more meaningful because of Ruth.

Preface

This is a story of love and devotion, hope and despair, anger and bitterness—and resolve; the resolve to do what's right, to live by the principles of love, duty, honor, and commitment. It's also a story about a heinous disease that takes no prisoners and for which there is no effective treatment and no cure. It's also an indictment of the institutions that pretend to help but fail to care for Alzheimer's tragic victims and their families, and of the too few places victims and their families can go for help and actually receive it. And lastly, it's a primer for present and future Alzheimer's caregivers. It provides a roadmap of what to expect and when you might expect it, which is complicated by getting what you might have expected when you least expect it. Stuff happens when you least expect or deserve it.

The story is an external narrative beginning with the initial medical testing, moving to a definitive diagnosis, and it chronicles the nine-year progression of care beginning in the home setting and moving to and through assisted living facilities. Along the way, I have provided detailed insights into the experiences that paralleled this external narrative in the hope that these insights, although specific, will resonate with readers and provide practical help and benefit to them and others.

Richard Masinton

There is, of course, an even more compelling and vastly more important narrative here. It is the internal narrative that is uniquely Dana's. Without this narrative there is nothing, but it is perhaps the cruelest paradox that her narrative is unknowable, even to those who love her the most deeply. We are forced to imagine her experience—the inexorable loss of her spirit, sparkling personality, and physical strength and vitality. The internal narrative is perhaps written on the walls of her heart, without memories but completely in the here and now. My best hope is that the care we provide Dana, to the fullest extent possible, is some protection and comfort for her experience also. It is only my hope for I can never truly know, but I remain steadfast in that hope nonetheless.

Unique to this book is an additional—and I hope significantly useful—narrative that speaks directly to you as this experience unfolds. It will be a frequent presence in the story. The comments in this narrative will appear in italics, and they have an important role to play. It is the voice of reason, common sense, experience, and insight—*Darn, why didn't I think of that?*—and it's going to have a lot to say. I hope you enjoy reading it and learning from it as much as I have in creating it. I just wish I'd met the voice of reason earlier because it could have saved me a lot of time, worry, and heartache. I came to understand this voice through painful experience. It gave me the test first, with the lesson to follow. You, on the other hand, will have the benefit of this voice's insight from the outset.

By way of introduction and background, let me introduce you to Dana as she was before Alzheimer's stole her from all of us. Even though there were earlier clues, at the time of her formal diagnosis, Dana was approximately fifty-six, which places her at the youngest edge of the age spectrum for patients with Alzheimer's and helps explain the incredible shock we felt then and live with to this day. Alzheimer's, which causes its sufferers to retreat into themselves irretrievably, could not have chosen a less suitable outward candidate for an inward retreat.

Tall, slender, and beautiful, with a willowy build and a confident, charming personality, Dana was a sparkling, social person who truly came alive in the company of others. Her well-honed social skills found their logical home in a highly successful career as a realtor, and her clients trusted her, often through multiple purchases for generations of their families. Dana had a natural elegance about her which immediately put people at ease in her company, and she always presented herself as a poised, put-together professional with a totally disarming smile. She was irresistible, but she didn't know it. She simply loved people and found them endlessly interesting.

Not surprisingly she had many close friends, but she also had a handful of beloved girlfriends who were like sisters to her and in whose company she had enjoyed many fun activities—and shenanigans—over many years. An effortless entertainer, she relished the opportunity to open her home and kitchen for shared meals and friendship. She was gifted with a pure, clear, soprano voice, and true to her nature she shared that gift of song in church, with friends, in moments of spontaneous joy, and, ironically, with folks in nursing homes. She adored the music of Broadway and was completely fascinated by birds, sprinkling her lovely garden with bird feeders and houses for nature's spectacular, winged beauties. She loved to travel, she loved a cosmopolitan before dinner, and she loved her family. Dana loved the world, and the world loved Dana. Most of all, Dana loved me. And then Dana's whole world changed forever.

This is the story of our experience with Alzheimer's disease. It is always and forever Dana's story, unique in every aspect, just as she was then and is today. Our journey thus far has also been unique because of the decisions that we made and the resources that were available to us. We are all different. Families make the best choices they can within a larger framework of moral judgments, financial circumstances, and available support structures. People with professional expertise in Alzheimer's will tell you at every opportunity that each patient is unique, but there are elements that are common enough that they form a map or at least an outline of the landscape of this terrible disease. It is my great hope that the story of Dana's unique journey can illuminate the landscape for at least one other person and their family and in doing so shed just a little light in the darkness.

The tragic and lingering story of Alzheimer's was described by Nancy Reagan as "the long goodbye" when she referred to President Reagan's battle with Alzheimer's. The struggle is long, but it is on the wrong side of goodbye. Others call the struggle a fade to gray. There is no fade. There are constant upheaval and uproar. There is turmoil, confrontation, loneliness, and despair. It is a fight to get through every hour of every day, with the only certainty being that tomorrow will be worse.

Introduction

by Ruth Ingall

Alzheimer's disease and related illnesses associated with cognitive decline or impairment are increasingly prevalent in the United States and worldwide. It is not an overstatement to say that it may be the disease of our generation, surpassing even cancer in terms of its impact on the nation's economy, its workforce, and our families. The Alzheimer's Association website, referencing data from 2013, states that Alzheimer's disease is "the sixth leading cause of death in the United States and the only one in the top ten without a means to prevent, cure, or slow its progression."

To underscore the significance of this, it's important to understand the dramatic increase in Alzheimer's diagnoses. While deaths from major diseases including cancer, heart disease, and stroke in the United States continue to significantly decline, between 2000 and 2010 deaths from Alzheimer's increased by a staggering sixty-eight percent.

Although Alzheimer's is not a normal part of the aging process, age is the disease's biggest risk factor. This is important because the number of people in the United States over sixty-five years old is expected to double by the year 2030, placing an enormous strain on the health care system at every level, the federal budget, and especially on America's families. If Alzheimer's merely continues the pattern it established during the first ten years of the millennium, the number of people living with Alzheimer's in 2050 will be sixteen million, with nearly one million new diagnoses annually.

In terms of the impact on our national budget, the Alzheimer's Association has projected that over the next forty years, caring for people with Alzheimer's will cost individuals, Medicare/Medicaid, and private health insurance companies $21 trillion. This is enough to completely pay off the current national debt and still send a check for $10,000 to every man, woman, and child in the United States. Clearly, this is a crisis of unprecedented proportions, and put simply, the graying of America threatens to bankrupt our country.

We will not begin to address this problem, much less meet the needs of patients and their families, until we recognize that Alzheimer's is a health care emergency and a public health epidemic. Unlike previous epidemics such as AIDS, polio, or tuberculosis, Alzheimer's disease is the unintended consequence of two things: A highly successful health care system, and increasing life spans for Americans in the twentieth and twenty-first centuries. Uniquely and cruelly, Alzheimer's can and does strike people whose underlying health may be excellent and who may have taken scrupulous care throughout their lives to minimize their risk factors for other serious, chronic medical conditions. Rapid expansion in medical knowledge combined with innovations in medical technology and diagnostics have significantly improved individual health care in the United States. We routinely survive medical episodes that would have caused our deaths in earlier times. We are living longer, and because of those extended lifespans, we are encountering diseases previously only associated with old age.

When the Social Security Act was signed into law in 1935, the average life expectancy in the United States was 59.9 years for a male, and 63.9 years for a female. The average life expectancy of a person who is currently sixty-five years old is 19.3 years, meaning they can reasonably assume they will live to be eighty-five years old.

Think back to your childhood; you can probably recall at least one elderly person in your family or among your acquaintances who had Alzheimer's disease. Now think about your life today; how many people do you know who are dealing with or have dealt with this dreadful illness? In all likelihood you can think of several people. Now extend that exercise to every family in the United States, and you can appreciate the size and scope of the new reality of Alzheimer's disease. We are spectacularly unprepared and tragically ill-equipped as a nation because we are facing a public health crisis without precedent in our history.

The words *public health crisis* are broad in scope and urgent in their implications, but do not make the mistake of depersonalizing this threat or assigning it to a governmental project or initiative for solutions or even short-term workarounds. In light of the statistics, it is absolutely essential to purchase long-term care insurance as part of a wise protection package for both individuals and families.

To be absolutely clear: The cost of Alzheimer's disease can easily devastate even the most prudent financial portfolio, especially when care in an assisted living facility or nursing home becomes necessary. Medicare and supplemental medical insurance do not cover these expenses. Medicaid can only be implemented after every personal financial resource has been exhausted, and waiting lists—as well as limited facility options—are common in many states. As with any personal insurance purchase, the price of policies is in direct proportion to age. So, the younger you are when you buy long-term care insurance, the lower the premium will be.

Many companies offer long-term care insurance as part of their employee benefits packages. These are almost always price-advantaged due to group membership through the employer and transfer to the employee—along with the responsibility for making the premium payments—upon retirement. Some companies will deduct long-term care premiums through payroll deduction. This decreases the impact on personal or family budgets. Deductions in each paycheck are not as noticeable as annual or semi-annual payments, so do include that question in your research.

As part of financial research and preparation for the possible impact of Alzheimer's, always ensure that you are familiar with nursing home eligibility qualifications and the provisions under Social Security Disability since both may factor into some of the most important financial decisions you can make, either for yourself or a family member.

We have all had the experience of misplacing something, forgetting a fact or detail, or losing our train of thought when distracted. Indeed, these things are commonplace in a modern, multi-tasking life. But memory loss that disrupts daily life is neither normal nor a typical part of the aging process. The Alzheimer's Association's website lists the following warning signs that may be helpful in determining whether further professional evaluation may be needed for you or a family member:

- Memory loss that disrupts daily life: Patients with Alzheimer's frequently forget recently learned information, important dates or events. They repeatedly ask for the same information, or they may suddenly rely on family members for things they used to handle on their own. In contrast, typical age-related change may be sometimes forgetting names or appointments but recalling them later.
- Challenges in planning or problem-solving: Patients may experience changes in their ability to develop or follow a plan, work with numbers, follow a recipe, or keep track of monthly bills. In contrast, typical age-related change might be making occasional errors when balancing a checkbook.
- Difficulty completing familiar tasks: People with Alzheimer's often find it hard to complete daily tasks such as driving to a familiar location, managing a budget at work, or remem-

bering the rules of a favorite game. In contrast, typical age-related change is occasionally needing help with settings on electronic devices.

- Confusion with time or place: People with Alzheimer's can lose track of dates, seasons, the passage of time, and may have trouble understanding something if it is not happening immediately. Sometimes they forget where they are or how they got there. In contrast, typical age-related change might be getting confused about the day of the week but figuring it out later.

- Trouble understanding visual images or spatial relationships: For some people vision problems are a sign of Alzheimer's. They may have difficulty reading, judging distance, and determining color or contrast. They may pass a mirror and not realize they are the person in the mirror. In contrast, typical age-related change might be vision changes related to cataracts.

- New problems with words or in speaking or writing: People with Alzheimer's may have trouble following or joining a conversation. They may stop in the middle of a conversation and have no idea how to continue, or they may repeat themselves. They may also struggle with vocabulary and finding the right word. In contrast, typical age-related change is sometimes having trouble finding the right word.

- Misplacing things and losing the ability to retrace steps: A person with Alzheimer's may put things in unusual places. They may lose things and be unable to retrace their steps to find them again. They may accuse others of stealing. This may occur more frequently over time. In contrast, typical age-related change might be misplacing things from time to time, such as a pair of glasses or the remote control.

- Decreased or poor judgment: People with Alzheimer's use poor judgment when dealing with money, giving large amounts to telemarketers. They may pay less attention to grooming or keeping themselves clean. In contrast, typical age-related change might be making a bad decision once in a while.

- Withdrawal from work or social activities: A person with Alzheimer's may have trouble keeping up with a favorite sports team or remembering how to complete a favorite hobby. They may also avoid being social because of the changes they have experienced. In contrast, typical age-related change is sometimes feeling weary of work, family, and social obligations.
- Changes in mood and personality: People with Alzheimer's can become confused, suspicious, depressed, fearful, or anxious. They may be easily upset at home, at work, with friends, or in places where they are out of their comfort zone. In contrast, typical age-related changes might be developing very specific ways of doing things and becoming irritated when a routine is disrupted.

The family is the central social point of life in the United States, and the family naturally feels the impact of any serious and chronic illness first. The clinical diagnosis of Alzheimer's for you or for someone you love is always a tremendous shock, regardless of—and sometimes in spite of—the number of subtle clues that may have preceded the formal announcement. Suddenly, the vague and disconnected symptoms lose their scattered patterns and click together like the last piece of a challenging jigsaw puzzle. The picture that once was composed of a thousand different pieces is now clear for all to see. And while there may be some element of relief in solving the puzzle, there is often also a cascade of other complicated emotions: Disbelief, questioning, anger, sadness, withdrawal, depression, and grief. When the diagnosis is reached, everyone in the family goes through each of them in their own way and on their own timetable and emotional terms.

In the short term, most families respond as they would in any crisis; they rally around and support each other. As the deeper reality sets in, families are challenged to find practical solutions to managing the needs and tasks that surround daily life. Those solutions are different for every family. There are literally hundreds of questions on a daily basis that a family must cope with, and it can feel completely overwhelming at times. Access to skilled, compassionate, emotionally supportive medical professionals is vital. Their guidance and practical advice, often based on extensive experience with other families dealing with Alzheimer's, is often the only bright light in a strange and bewildering landscape. Likewise, comfort and advice from a member of the clergy with a longstanding knowledge of the family can sometimes help immensely.

Find information and people in whom you can place your trust, and reach out to them. Knowledge is power here, and shared knowledge in the care of the patient and the family is essential.

While the emotional impact of Alzheimer's on the family is significant, the financial effect can be profound or even catastrophic. The Alzheimer's Association estimates that "one in seven American workers is an active or former caregiver for someone with Alzheimer's ... and the effect on the workplace is simply astounding." Moreover, 15 million workers are currently unpaid caregivers for people with Alzheimer's, a number that will certainly grow as the predicted incidence of the disease increases by 30 percent between now and 2025. In practical terms, 15 million people are providing 17 billion hours of their time, which represents a commercial caregiving value of more than $202 billion per year. Those are 2016's figures. There is no reason to believe that they will decrease in the foreseeable future.

A landmark report released by the Alzheimer's Association in 2013, *Workplace Options and the Alzheimer's Association*, polled workers who were also unpaid caregivers at home and found that:

- 69 percent had to arrive late to work, leave early, or take off time during the day;
- 32 percent had to take a leave of absence;
- 20 percent said their job performance suffered to the point of possible dismissal.

The increasing incidence of Alzheimer's—one in eight Americans age 65 or older has the disease—means there are layers of productivity impact on the economy. Lost productivity caused by family members leaving the workforce to care for Alzheimer's patients represents a loss of expertise, a loss of productivity, and a loss to business owners and shareholders. Most significantly, the transition of an employee, whether full or part-time, to the role of unpaid caregiver is always accompanied by high levels of emotional stress and sometimes by clinical depression.

These facts are hard to read, especially when they affect you personally. Dealing with facts on paper and living with their reality in all aspects of daily life are two completely different things. As with any serious medical diagnosis, it is important to take the time to process information and understand the personal implications—whether you are a patient or a caregiver—as well as the broader implications for your immediate and extended family, your finances, and daily life.

This impact of an Alzheimer's diagnosis and the accompanying cascade of emotions such as anger, disbelief, withdrawal, and depression are all normal reactions to having your reality permanently changed. For every question that is answered, it seems that at least five more spring up, especially in the turbulent period immediately following diagnosis. Be assertive in seeking the answers that you need. Ask about things you don't understand, and don't assume that your questions are unimportant. Bear in mind that people with knowledge and skill in Alzheimer's are overwhelmingly ready and willing to share what they know with you. Above all else, know that there are no stupid questions. Everyone benefits when everyone knows.

It is important that you do not allow yourself or your Alzheimer's patient to be unduly hurried. Pay close attention if someone you interact with for care or treatment appears to be in a rush. Speak slowly and carefully with them. The modern medical environment can be overwhelming even for healthy people, so it is easy to appreciate how frightening it can feel for patients with Alzheimer's.

Choose physicians and other members of the medical team who give freely of their time, who ask whether all of your questions have been answered, and who ask whether there is anything else they can do for you before they leave your appointment. The highest quality care always takes place in an unhurried atmosphere. Likewise, don't hesitate to routinely ask for a brief, verbal summary from your health care providers at the end of appointments. This is especially helpful in making sure that everyone has heard and understood the same things and has a clear understanding of the next steps in the patient's care. Take notes if that is something you like to do so that you have the key points easily at hand if someone has a question later. This simple technique can also be very helpful in relaying important information to family members not present at medical appointments.

Trust and respect are essential elements in healthy relationships, and especially in therapeutic relationships. Alzheimer's is a complex disease that causes suffering to millions of patients and their families. The burden and suffering of Alzheimer's should never include a relationship with a physician or other care provider with whom you feel uncomfortable or where there may simply be incompatible personalities. The ideal therapeutic relationship should feel positive and helpful, not strained, confused, or awkward. No physician is so medically brilliant that they can afford to ignore the simple and profound humanity in caring for sick patients.

If, after a reasonable time and considerable effort, you feel that the fit is not right between you and your physician, by all means make a change. Do it respectfully and constructively, but do it in the confident hope that another physician may be a better fit for you, your patient, and your circumstances. Insurance networks, geographic location, and available alternatives for care from medical specialists are all important factors in these decisions, so be sure to research your options going forward before making a change.

You also need to maintain a healthy relationship with yourself if you are the primary caregiver for a loved one with Alzheimer's. Using the oft-quoted example from the safety briefing on commercial aircraft, remember to secure your own oxygen mask before attempting to help others. Realize the importance of brief breaks in the ongoing responsibility of care—especially for someone you love—and find respite support so that you can refresh your mind as well as take care of essential medical, dental, and other personal appointments for yourself. Think of those breaks as a chance to clear your mind and catch your breath. Establish a routine so that you do not succumb to feelings of guilt when you leave for a short while.

There are exceptions to every generalization, but it is very common for Alzheimer's patients to reach a point in the progression of the disease where care in the home may no longer be practical. The reasons are many and varied. Safety in the physical environment for both patient and family can be problematic, management of complex medical issues may require close supervision by trained personnel, and the logistics of maintaining a normal life may become overwhelming if not impossible. Whatever the individual situation may be, the time may well come when care in an assisted living facility or nursing home becomes a matter of sensible urgency. Available financial resources become a determining factor when and if this time comes. If a private nursing home or assisted living facility is beyond the budget, Medicaid facilities may be an option.

Most of the important decisions we make as consumers are guided by price, quality, and value. This is something we're not always conscious of. We search for bargains on some things but not on others, especially where we have definite preferences or favorite brands. The world of nursing homes is a universe unto itself, and we enter that universe on the most unfavorable consumer terms possible because we need to make an expensive purchasing decision very often in a short timeframe. In most cases we have little or no experience with the range of products on sale and even less access to meaningful information about the quality of either the physical facility or more importantly the quality of nursing care. A 2001 report, *Regulating US Nursing Homes*, noted, "More than 1.6 million Americans live in nursing homes, most of them elderly, frail, and vulnerable persons.... Because of their physical or mental infirmity and their dependence on their caregivers, they are often not able to act as assertive, well-informed consumers."

Most people are aware of nursing homes and the important role they have in the delivery of healthcare in the United States. Comparatively few people have any real knowledge of the nursing home industry in their communities unless they, a family member, or someone they know has needed care in a nursing home or assisted living facility. As previously discussed, medical insurance does not cover nursing home accommodation. Many people might be surprised and alarmed to learn that the cost of nursing home accommodation is similar living at an expensive hotel on a long-term basis. Amounts vary from state to state, but a reasonable working figure is around $250 per day or $7,400 per month. That is more expensive than tuition, room and board and fees at Harvard, which was $60,659 for the 2015–16 academic year. When you consider the time, financial planning, and care in the selection that goes into sending a student to an elite educational environment such as Harvard, it literally staggers the mind to realize that almost no advance thought or preparation goes into decisions about placing patients, much less people we love, in nursing homes. Remember, you are going to Harvard for four years. Someone is quite likely to stay in a nursing home for the rest of their life.

According to *Regulating US Nursing Homes*, "The great majority of nursing homes (93 percent) are operated by the private sector; 67 percent of those by for-profit organizations, including a growing number of large corporations whose facilities house thousands of residents."

That means that roughly three out of every four nursing homes are for-profit entities. While these facilities are responsible for complying with state and federal regulations, they measure their ongoing success through profits and return on investment for their stakeholders.

The regulatory structure of the nursing home industry in the United States is conceptually simple but administratively complex, which creates the most serious problems for patients and their families. The problems often begin with the selection of a nursing home. Sometimes the choice is made by a hospital discharge planner, sometimes the family receives a referral from a friend or relative to a facility in their community, and sometimes the choice is made after a brief and often urgent search among local nursing homes.

The National Care Planning Council has some wise and sensible advice on its website about selecting a nursing home: "Call all the facilities in your area and ask for bed rates. Also, ask about staff turnover, age of the facility...whether it is a chain, locally owned or non-profit and whether they offer the level of care that you need. You can eliminate a number of facilities before you take the next step of an inspection tour."

The most critical piece of advice during inspection tours, based on the narrative in this book and the experiences of many others, is to look beyond the wrapping paper and the marketing brochures when evaluating a nursing home. This is emotionally counterintuitive since we want and need to provide the best we can for those we love, especially in their time of need.

However, as the National Care Planning Council notes, "The newness of a facility and the amenities say nothing about the quality of care. Many older facilities have lower fixed costs and may be able to give quality care at lower rates, even if the surroundings are not so spiffy. The staff and administration are key to a quality nursing home stay, not the physical surroundings. A good indicator of quality is how long staff members have been with the facility. Long tenures usually mean job satisfaction...always ask about tenure and turnover rates."

Your numerous questions have been asked and answered, you've taken the tours, and you've selected the nursing home. It will either be a good decision—in which case be thankful every day for the unique confluence of circumstances that made that happen—or it will be a decision you will struggle with daily.

The poignant and powerful story of Dana's encounters with nursing homes will illustrate some of their numerous pitfalls and shortcomings. The discussion here will focus on the reasons why nursing homes—and the experiences of residents and their families—are unlikely to improve in the near future. This discussion of faults and failings is intended to light the way for those who follow, to minimize the disappointment when challenges arise, and to provide strategies and techniques that may be helpful. Above all, the emphasis is on removing the powerless feeling that so many people describe when advocating for quality nursing home care on behalf of someone they love.

The biggest problem is this: In the current high demand/limited supply market for nursing home accommodation, there is absolutely no financial incentive for nursing homes to compete for residents or to deliver on care promises once a prospective resident moves in. This is particularly true of large corporate nursing homes. Remember, their first responsibility is to their stakeholders, not their patients. Never fall into the trap of believing that the best interest of your loved one is uppermost in the minds of people in those huge organizational charts. Their size often makes accountability difficult to establish, and responsibility is almost impossible to enforce when it comes to problems or issues in two critical areas: Medical-nursing and business-financial. A third area—activities related to daily living—can be problematic and annoying, but is not as critical.

Medical-nursing issues in nursing homes are also the result of supply and demand, particularly where profitability is concerned, because a quality nursing staff is difficult to attract, train, and retain. The glossy, gorgeous marketing brochure probably describes the nursing care—the primary reason for a nursing home's existence—as *highly skilled, trained, caring, and attentive.* In reality, the majority of nursing home care in the United States is provided by overworked and underpaid certified nurse assistants (CNA) and/or licensed practical nurses (LPN). They in turn usually work under the supervision of a registered nurse (RN) who receives direction from a physician that is either the medical director of the nursing home or the patient's personal physician. In some settings there is no RN, so CNAs and LPNs report directly—usually by phone or email—to physicians for guidance in the care of their patients.

Understaffing in nursing homes, in training levels, and patient-nurse ratios are widespread and reflect a national nursing shortage as well as a deliberate attempt to maximize profits. As a result, staff morale in nursing homes is often low. Staff turnover is frequently high, especially in facilities with poor management, and the nursing work is physically and emotionally demanding. Advocates or family members for anyone in a nursing home need to understand these realities and form close working relationships with the nursing staff charged with the care of your loved one.

These nurses are in constant, daily contact with your patient. Make sure to create and maintain an open, respectful, and constructive conversation with them about your ongoing and changing needs. Pay meticulous attention to the care plan. This is the agreed-upon basis for medical-nursing care and is an extension of the contract between the patient and the facility. Medications, dosages, treatments, daily care, and other therapeutic interactions such as physical therapy are all documented in the care plan. Failure to execute the care plan accurately is a serious matter with the potential for patient harm. The responsibility for checking and re-checking the quality of nursing care falls squarely on the advocate or representative of a patient in a nursing home—you.

Sadly, there have been instances where patient neglect or abuse has occurred. According to the National Care Planning Council, "Abuse is not only physical assault or threats, but can also be such things as improper use of restraints, failure to feed or give water, failure to bathe, improper care resulting in pressure sores, or allowing a patient to remain in a soiled diaper or bed linen."

Thirty-six states have a patient bills of rights. Always know the details that apply to your state, and make absolutely sure that your patient's rights are upheld.

The establishment of a good relationship with the nursing staff is essential to both the patient's welfare and the family's peace of mind. After the initial settling-in phase of residency, the business and financial aspect of nursing homes begins, and a new and different range of problems and challenges await.

Nothing—repeat, nothing—will get and keep the attention of the corporation that runs a nursing home like an unpaid bill. The only real leverage and control that a consumer of nursing care services has is the power of the purse. Be absolutely clear-eyed about this; it is first and foremost a business relationship bound by a legal contract for the exchange of services in return for payment. Patients whose expenses are reimbursed by Medicaid do not have the same leverage as patients whose expenses are paid privately. But in either case, it is entirely appropriate to refuse payment for contractual services that are not provided or stated expectations that are not met. Do not be intimidated by the lack of alternative accommodations. While it may be too expensive or impractical to move to another facility, it is never appropriate to accept care that fails to meet the standards stated in the residency contract.

It sounds straightforward in concept; in practice it can be confusing, infuriating, time-consuming, and emotionally exhausting. The market forces that deliver poorly paid and exhausted nurses to your facility also deliver inexperienced bookkeepers and overextended, incompetent managers. Moreover, both of them report to a distant, uninvolved, and usually unconcerned business hierarchy that is unlikely to take your call or answer your urgent question should a serious problem arise. That is why families and trustees of privately paying patients should never agree to automatic payments for nursing home care, no matter how strenuously the facility's management urges them to for reasons of convenience. It may be a problem for trustees who want payments made in a timely manner, but it's important to have leverage for accountability. Before paying, make sure that your patient has received every item or service that is listed on the monthly statement and included in the care plan, and be diligent and determined in seeking a reasonable remedy or account adjustment if any deficiencies are found. It's unlikely the facility will try to evict the patient if the reason for nonpayment is their failure to perform under the contract.

As mentioned earlier, any problems related to the activities of daily living that arise will require both time and attention to resolve effectively. These may include behavioral issues by your patient such as personality changes and aggressive behavior towards staff or fellow residents or, conversely, verbal abuse or bullying toward the patient.

Nursing home activities can present challenges. The same patient who previously enjoyed them may derive less value from them as their medical needs change over time, so be prepared to make adjustments based on your observations as well as recommendations from staff whose opinions and experience you trust.

Alzheimer's patients often lose track of personal items, such as eyeglasses, so it is wise to have extra supplies on hand in case the need arises. Likewise, clothing and laundry items can be misplaced, especially in a large facility, so be aware of that possibility. It is generally unwise to have expensive or irreplaceable personal possessions in any group residence setting. Use your best judgment about how to manage the risks associated with any potential losses.

Mnemosyne, the ancient Greek goddess of memory, was considered one of the most powerful goddesses of her time. Memory was seen as the gift that allows us to reason, to predict and anticipate outcomes; it's what distinguishes us from the other creatures in the animal world, what makes us uniquely us. Alzheimer's steals that gift. It is a thief that claims its precious trophies slowly and at tremendous and unbearable cost.

In attempting to describe the experience of caring for a loved one with Alzheimer's, other writers have used terms such as *the long goodbye*, and indeed, the title of this book, *Fade to Gray*, may suggest a gentle dimming of a life's light. In reality, the clinical and emotional progress of Alzheimer's disease is far more turbulent and unpredictable than gentle metaphors may indicate or that our fondest hopes would wish for. The inspiration for this book lies in the author's heartfelt hope that by shining a light on one person's journey through Alzheimer's, the journey of others through this complex landscape may be made less burdensome, even if only through the knowledge that someone else understands.

God bless all families who love someone struggling with Alzheimer's, the dedicated doctors and nurses who care for them daily, and the brilliant researchers who constantly search for a cure.

Chapter 1:
Chocolate Cake

Two years prior to diagnosis ...

Dana and I had worked all our adult lives. Me for forty-plus years as a professional manager and Dana for more than thirty years as a realtor. Dana was fifty-five years old; I was sixty-six. We were approaching the time in our lives when we started to think about not going to work every day although I avoided the word *retirement*. I had been asked and agreed to stay on with my company beyond the time I normally would have considered retiring, and Dana still enjoyed selling houses. We did, however, think from time to time that when we quit working every day, we would spend more time in Arizona and more time traveling and doing the things that normal people think about doing when they retire.

Even so, we were starting to spend increasingly more time in our Scottsdale, Arizona getaway. Each time we arrived in Scottsdale, we found ourselves relaxing and thinking that this was the way we intended to enjoy our time together. We decided to get out of our home base in Kansas City and go to Scottsdale for a couple of weeks and really relax. I was tired, and Dana had just completed the sale of the Cohen's house, which had taken a great deal of her time and appeared to be a very stressful transaction for her. We arrived in Scottsdale, settled into our condo, got up in the morning, and went to have breakfast at the Wildflower Bread Company.

We ate breakfast out almost every day when we were in Scottsdale. It was fun, relaxing, and a great break from getting up early every morning, grabbing a cup of coffee, and rushing off to work. We would typically spend two or three hours at breakfast. I would read the *Wall Street Journal*, get up-to-date on the sports world, catch up on emails, and do a little Internet surfing. Dana would do a couple of extremely difficult Sudoku puzzles and visit with any warm body who might wander by our table. She particularly enjoyed the servers, knew their names, their children's ages, the breed of their dog, and where and how they spent their leisure life. She would even occasionally jump up and help them bus a table. Dana never met a stranger. She could visit with a post.

This outing for breakfast was not any different from the hundreds that came before. It ended on the usual high note as we drove back home. When we arrived at the condo, I went to my office alcove next to the kitchen to review our investments and catch up on some other personal business we had let slide over the past several weeks while attending to our day jobs. Dana sat at the kitchen island to pay bills and reconcile her bank account. Time slipped away from me when I worked on our investments, not because there was so much to work on, but because I realized that I was approaching the time when we would begin drinking lake water rather than river water, so I was always mindful about keeping track of the water level in the lake.

I don't know how long I had been sitting at my desk but enough time had passed that I became aware Dana was struggling with something concerning the household finances. When I asked what was up, she said that she was frustrated by the bank's inability to keep our account straight; the bank had made several mistakes, and she couldn't get her checking account to agree with the bank statement. She was clearly exasperated.

I sat down at the kitchen island to try and help. No wonder she could not reconcile it—her check register looked like it had been dipped into an inkwell. She had left trails of going through the register repeatedly in an attempt to reconcile the account. There were highlighting, notes, asterisks, scribbles, check marks, and all kinds of corrections everywhere. I couldn't even read it.

I retrieved the account online and backtracked several months to a point of near-agreement with the bank. Using that as a starting point, I worked forward and noticed a pattern of duplicated payments—some automatic bank drafts, some not—and I started finding instances of bills paid in a purely random fashion. The account was a complete mess; there was no reason to think that the online statement and the check register related to the same account.

I moved onto the paper bill file and found numerous unpaid, past due bills. It was unlike Dana to have a mess like this. She was an organized, bright person. She had been a math and business major in college, and paying bills and keeping the family account straight had never been an issue with her. She could do it with her eyes shut. Yet there was now a serious problem, and she was very frustrated and upset over it. Sensing this, I started a clean page in the register and reconciled the account hoping for a clean start, all the while worrying that there were people out there who had not been paid or had been paid more than once.

While troubled at the time, I didn't initially attach serious significance to the episode because she had been extremely busy at work with the Cohen transaction. But I thought back to the episode over the next few days and connected it with an unease I had semiconsciously felt over the past weeks and months that maybe Dana had changed a little. Uncharacteristically, work had been bothering her, and she seemed somewhat distant in a way that was hard to explain. It was nothing I could put my finger on, but it was there.

This is where it starts, folks. Looking back, it's so clear and obvious. Living through it at the time, not so much. Those CAN'T PUT MY FINGER ON IT; SOMETHING IS DIFFERENT OR DISTANT IN A WAY THAT'S HARD TO EXPLAIN *moments are* REAL *and* IMPORTANT. *When you encounter them, please don't ignore them. That little voice telling you that something isn't right is* ABSOLUTELY CORRECT. *The path is always clearer looking through the rearview mirror than viewing it through the windshield.*

We had discussed her feeling a little different, not quite right, and being irritable at times; that maybe menopause was taking its toll. The hot flashes were there. We had talked about the doctors changing her hormone patch—I don't remember whether they had adjusted the dosage, taken it away, or doubled it. Maybe the bill paying situation was the culmination of too many or too few hormones, the aging process, or whatever.

Over the next several days, while we were enjoying the Valley of the Sun, I kept reflecting on what had seemed a few days ago to be a problem with Dana's bank account. I recalled things that—had I thought about them long enough at the time—might have indicated a change in Dana. Now remember, this is an organized, smart woman. But on reflection, she often misplaced her glasses or couldn't find her car keys, and when I tried to help, she would get short and irritated with me. I'd eventually find those misplaced items in unusual places—her glasses in a cabinet in the laundry room or the car keys in a dresser drawer.

This is what I was talking about earlier, except on a practical level. Everyone misplaces things from time to time, but a pattern of frequently losing things is something to watch out for, particularly when the items show up in weird places.

Not so long ago she had made a Mississippi Mud cake for my birthday—my favorite—and it turned out inedible. When she tasted it, she couldn't believe that something had gone wrong. Maybe it was the oven, maybe something else. Then I recalled other things she had cooked that didn't turn out right. Perhaps it was the result of her being busy and distracted, but perhaps it was something else. Things began to piece together.

I delicately started talking to Dana about these occurrences and discovered that these very things had been on her mind, and she had been worried about them. She knew that she had been misplacing things, forgetting things, making mistakes, reacting more irritably, and not feeling quite right. The first few times we talked about it, she became upset, emotional, and cried. She brought up the Cohen real estate transaction and admitted that she had trouble negotiating the deal, couldn't keep the numbers straight. She broke down and said she had done hundreds of real estate deals and contracts and never had a problem before, but this time she needed help from her broker to complete the contracts and close the deal.

That she was aware of it and troubled by it confirmed to me that there might be something more seriously wrong than simply a hormone patch or a hot flash. After more reflection, I realized there had been subtle clues sprinkled throughout the previous two or three years that had appeared disconnected but now assumed a compelling and urgent relevance. It dated back to when Dana was only fifty-two or fifty-three years old. We agreed that we should visit with Dr. Monaco, our physician in Kansas City, and try to find out whether this was a physical, medical, or stress-related problem.

A day or two later the chocolate cake incident came out in our discussions. It embarrassed her, and on a high note she offered to make a new cake for me, so we could enjoy it in Arizona before we had to go back to work. That may have been the turning point in how we were going to approach the next days, weeks, months, and years. She started to make the cake and simply could not even begin to do it. Even with the recipe and my help, she was unable to follow the simplest steps in a familiar process that at one time had been effortless and enjoyable for her. The sequential steps of following a recipe were simply overwhelming. I gently offered to help in a way that wouldn't embarrass her or make her frustrated. We made the cake and enjoyed it, but it was the last one that ever successfully came out of her oven. At that point I decided we should cut our trip to Scottsdale short and quickly get an appointment with Dr. Monaco to try and make some sense of the signs we had noticed over the past months and years—and the significance of those signs.

Chapter 2:
Not Too Alarmed

We got back to Kansas City, went to see Dr. Monaco, and explained to him our concerns as best we could from both of our perspectives—mine observational and Dana's from the inside out. We talked about her misplacing things, fumbling around in the kitchen, struggling with recipes, her frustration with her business, her disaster with the family checkbook, and on and on. We told him all the things we could remember that had been happening.

He gave her the standard internal medicine annual physical with blood work and EKG, and on top of that he gave her a short neurological exam—reflexes, tracking, balance, and the like. Then he asked her to sit down because he wanted to ask her some questions, something I had not seen before. He asked her what day it was, what time it was, what month it was, where she was, where she lives, and what county we were in.

He asked her to draw the face of a clock and to draw the hands to indicate three o'clock. He drew a cube with a pencil and asked her to do the same thing right next to it. He gave her several words to memorize and explained he would ask her to repeat them back to him sometime later. He asked her to count down from one hundred by sevens. He asked her to write a sentence. He showed her pictures of four presidents and asked her if she knew who they were. That brought a smile to her face because she clearly knew Gerald Ford, Ronald Reagan, Bill Clinton, and George W. Bush. She laughed and said: "Who wouldn't know who these people are?"

In the main, she answered all the questions, except for when the doctor returned to the words he had asked her to remember. She could not recall one or two of them. The cube was also a problem for her, which struck me as strange, especially since his example was right next to where he wanted her to duplicate it. When she was counting backward by seven from one hundred, she slowed down after the first few. That wasn't like her. She was really good with numbers, but it had been a long day, and I didn't really think anything of it.

This test is going to show up often, like a nosy neighbor or a bad dream. It's called the Mini-Mental State Examination (MMSE), and you can find a handy-dandy copy of it in the Appendix. You're going to get to know it and loathe it. And you're not even the one taking the test! The one taking the test will loathe it as much as you do, but also grow to be afraid of it. Brutal truth. Know thine enemy, folks.

When I asked the doctor about the exercise, he explained it was testing mental acuity. Little did I know then that in the ensuing years when given the same test and shown those pictures, she would go from laughing about *Who wouldn't know who these people are* to knowing three and guessing on the fourth, to knowing two, to not having the slightest idea who any of them were.

Dr. Monaco scored the test and said that he scored her right on the borderline between being OK and the first step of maybe you've slipped a bit. That was our introduction to the MMSE, an exercise Dana would go through dozens of times over the next few years and become increasingly terrified of.

The doctor wasn't alarmed by the results but urged us to be prudent and cover our bases. He wanted Dana to go to see a neurologist for a consultation and second opinion. After some thought he referred us to Midwest Medical Center to see a young female neurologist, Dr. Mary Weller, who he thought was good and someone Dana could relate to. He was aware that Dana didn't like to go to doctors as evidenced by her reaction when he suggested we get a second opinion, and he thought Dr. Weller would get Dana over that hurdle. He had referred other patients to her with good outcomes.

We then talked about menopause, hormones, and other medical and environmental issues including stress and work-related factors. We left his office feeling neither high nor low. We drove directly to the Bristol restaurant where I ordered a lemon drop martini and Dana ordered her regular cosmopolitan. We discussed going to Midwest Med and that Dr. Monaco was going to arrange the appointment. He said that he would call us when the appointment had been arranged. We didn't know if it would be next week or next month. For the time being, we were happy enough sipping on our martinis.

Chapter 3:
Mincemeat

While waiting for Dana's referral to Midwest Med, we tried to resume our normal life. I didn't know what was going through Dana's mind, but as time passed I became more comfortable with the idea we were going down a path that would tell us we had nothing to worry about. And if something was wrong with Dana, we were doing everything we should by going to the doctor and seeking multiple opinions and were on the right path to a resolution. That our doctor thought there was probably nothing serious going on reassured us.

However, as the days wore on, I became less sure. Dana's behavior either became more erratic or my heightened awareness made me more concerned with each bizarre thing she did or said. I continued to reflect on the previous couple of years and saw there was a progression of behavior. I was able to start connecting the dots. The more I thought about it and the visit with the doctor, the more I began thinking this was something more serious than the change of life. Our doctor, while a highly-trained professional, only saw Dana for an hour or so, and during that time had listened to whatever she and I could cobble together about what we had been experiencing. But I lived with her day in and day out and was seeing and experiencing something that just wasn't right. For the next few weeks, I was preoccupied with what I saw and piecing it together with what I remembered having seen in the recent past; however, I was hopeful we would find some answers and a resolution at the Midwest Medical Center.

See? Something's JUST NOT RIGHT. As you live this, the building blocks seem to fall more into place each day. Start making notes. Keep a diary if you think that will help. It's not your imagination. Some serious advice here: Now would be an excellent time to make sure that all your affairs (financial and legal/estate) are in order. If all is well, you're in great shape. If not, you need to act while your loved one is still legally capable of making these important decisions. You will be glad you did this no matter what the outcome.

Several weeks after the referral was made, the call came and the appointment was made for Dana to go to Midwest Medical Center. She was apprehensive, but I had no idea what might have been going through her mind. I could only imagine that she was concerned and probably frightened. That, combined with her dislike of going to doctors, made for a tense drive to the medical center. Our conversation revolved around her saying she didn't know why we were going and that we just needed to balance her hormones. It's unfortunate that the Department of Neurology at the Midwest Medical Center was housed in a building that looked a like a barracks from World War II and was decorated and furnished accordingly. While the interior might have been updated since the Big War, it looked worn and dingy and relatively uninviting. The musty smell and dingy appearance did not set a very good tone with Dana. The hallways were narrow, and the incandescent lights reflecting off drab hospital paint made the trek through the facility ominous and depressing.

We met Dr. Weller, whose appearance was right out of the '60s. She was young with bright eyes, short, curly hair and was dressed in a long skirt that was a throwback to Woodstock. But she was friendly and cheerful and, to the extent possible under the conditions, made Dana feel somewhat comfortable with her soft and gentle approach.

The first item on her agenda was to turn Dana over to someone else. I don't recall whether this person was an assistant, social worker, or psychometrician, but Dr. Weller told Dana that she wanted to spend some time visiting with me. That did not sit well with Dana. One of the eccentricities she had acquired over the previous few months was paranoia about things that might be going on, and she feared situations where she thought people were talking about her behind her back.

After Dana had left, the doctor spent a good deal of time with me asking about my take on Dana and what I had seen and experienced. She had already talked with our Dr. Monaco but wanted to get my side of the story. I'd had several weeks to think about Dana since our visit with our family doctor, so the things I had seen or experienced with Dana were now fresh in my mind as I answered Dr. Weller's series of questions.

Progression: Dana started having some memory issues after the onset of menopause. At the time I would have probably described it as forgetfulness. Dana had either started, stopped, or changed taking hormones several months earlier, and to me, the forgetfulness and confusion seemed to be getting worse rather than better as she progressed through menopause. I observed that Dana sometimes functioned pretty well until she had trouble doing or remembering something. That's when her personality changed and things would fall apart.

Dana had also become increasingly irascible and not as bright and cheery as she had always been - some things seemed to fluster and confuse her. On occasion, she had anxiety or panic attacks that manifested in a frantic mood and an urge to throw up, along with a period of serious confusion and an inability to communicate coherently. These episodes would last for perhaps five or ten minutes. They would go away as fast as they came, but Dana was left exhausted, with no memory of the episode at all.

Personality change is real. That person you thought you knew so well can and will change right before your eyes into someone completely strange and unexpected. The quiet person becomes loud and rude; the outspoken person becomes silent and withdrawn. And the inability to remember these episodes, outbursts, or spells is absolutely typical of Alzheimer's patients. Try not to be alarmed, even though it will be deeply shocking and unpredictable.

Dana was spending what I thought was an inordinate amount of time reminiscing about her mother, father, and grandmother—particularly her mother Bonnie, a nurse. She seemed to mention them almost every day. After our wonderful cat, Amstel, had died about a year ago, Dana and I both took it hard, but she had not really recovered from it. She would talk about her kitty Amstel all the time.

Anxiety: Dana sometimes seemed anxious and at other times seemed like there were no problems whatsoever. She seemed to be somewhat better at our second home in Arizona than when she was at home in Kansas. We thought that might be because the Arizona home was smaller and less stressful in the absence of her children and other family issues; it was more of a vacation home for Dana.

Dana was more tearful than usual and didn't have the energy she once had. Dana also seemed more withdrawn socially, which was a significant change because she was a social animal. She had always lit up the room when she entered; however, recently the light was not so bright when she was present.

Sleep habits: Dana retired relatively early and seemed to sleep well. I had noticed that sometimes during the night she would have occasional episodes of spasmodic twitching, but they did not wake her.

Diet and alcohol consumption: Dana ate well and enjoyed alcoholic beverages; her favorites being a cosmopolitan or a glass or two of good wine. We had a wine cellar and would enjoy a glass or two of wine most evenings at and around dinner time.

Technology: Dana was having difficulty using her new cell phone and retrieving her voicemails, and it had been some time since she could manipulate the television remote without becoming confused and frustrated.

Memory: Dana and I could go to a movie and dinner, and by the next day she occasionally would not recall either the movie or the dinner from the night before. I thought Dana could recall events generally, but I couldn't tell if she could recall all the details. Over the past year or so, Dana had acquired an obsession for keeping notes and lists. She seemed to be making lists of everything, and the parts of the house where she spent most of her time had Post-It Notes everywhere. It was clear to me that this obsession with lists and notes indicated Dana knew that she was struggling.

The use of lists and various reminders is an important clue. In the early phases of Alzheimer's disease, you may notice your loved one making unusually heavy use of lists and other reminders to maintain control over routine things; and indeed, the routine nature of the lists may obscure their clinical significance. The important difference between normal shopping lists and diary entries and those of Alzheimer's patients is that their lists do not reassure them. For example, immediately after completing one list or reminder, they will duplicate it JUST TO BE SURE. And of course, they sometimes misplace the list, which magnifies the panic and uncertainty—yet another clue to watch for.

One of the more bizarre occurrences happened on the day before our last trip to Arizona. Dana went to the supermarket and bought a ton of groceries for our house in Kansas City. She would go shopping but would often forget to buy needed items. I had observed her mop the kitchen floor and then a couple of hours later mop it again. She either didn't think it was clean enough or had forgotten that she had just done it.

Dana struggled to follow recipes but always remembered to fill the bird feeders with seed. She didn't read as much as she used to, and I thought that was probably because she was unable to remember what she had just read from time to time. Interestingly enough, Dana did Sudoku puzzles every day and made a point to solve the most difficult ones.

Appointments: Dana rarely had problems with this partly because she checked her calendar about every twenty minutes. I'd also noticed that she was rarely oriented to the date or day of the week but always knew what month and year it was. I concluded that Dana probably would have problems with multitasking or handling multiple stimuli, which was something that she could easily handle not so very long ago.

Each one of the preceding discussion items with the doctor is a behavior pattern that may be associated with Alzheimer's disease. Being oriented to month and year, but not day or date; repeating simple chores; shopping for groceries immediately prior to leaving town; the inability to perform sequential tasks, such as following the steps in a favorite recipe; and frustration with personal technology such as phones and television controls are all indicators of significant change in the ability to navigate the activities of daily living. It is not uncommon, however, for some higher-order skills such as puzzles to follow a different pattern. Be alert also to the loss of ability to follow the plot in movies and books, especially in someone who is an avid reader or movie-goer.

After our visit, the doctor invited Dana and her assistant back into the room with us where we spent a few minutes chatting and exchanging small talk. At that point, Dr. Weller asked me to leave the room, and she spent time with Dana and examined her. After she had visited with Dana, she called me back into the room and explained to us that among other things, she had given Dana a neurobehavioral evaluation—Dana's second exposure to an MMSE. She went through the details of the examination and diagnosed Dana as having memory loss due to stress, anxiety, depression, and alcohol use. She suggested Dana abstain from alcohol for a month.

I was expected to walk away thinking that if we worked on reducing Dana's stress, kept her out of situations that caused anxiety, managed her depression, and limited the amount of good wine she drank, then she'd be back to normal, and we could get on with our lives and enjoy our retirement together.

Not!

Dr. Weller wanted Dana to return in two to three months but in the meantime made an appointment for her to undergo a comprehensive cognitive evaluation with a psychologist and to receive MRI testing to examine the inside of the brain for any missed clues.

Our first two steps—the visit to our family physician followed by a referral to a specialist—are completely reasonable when a medical issue arises. At the end of the specialty referral, it's accurate to say I felt that the yield to this point was very questionable. We still had no idea what we were dealing with, and we had no clear guidelines on what to do or what we could expect to happen next.

I called our family doctor and expressed my frustration with the Midwest Medical Center visit and the ensuing diagnosis. I told him I doubted we were any closer to understanding what was going on. He could only reassure me to continue the path we were on. He also wanted us to see a psychiatrist.

In summary, we had seen the family physician, been evaluated by the specialist, were going to have a comprehensive neurological examination and MRI, and we're going to see a psychiatrist. We were to gather all this information and go back to see the neurologist at the Midwest Medical Center. In the meantime Dana continued to struggle, was now starting to have serious headaches, and was sick and tired of seeing doctors.

The trip to the psychiatrist was, well, a trip to a psychiatrist. We once again had to go through the history of our experiences, take another MMSE—which indicated that Dana was less than perfect and maybe a little worse than the last time she took it—and talk about the neurologist's findings. We came away from the visit with instructions to try not to be stressed or depressed or drink too much alcohol. The psychiatrist's conclusion was that he wasn't going to be of much help. In short, it was a waste of time and money and another pick at Dana's doctor scab that was getting more sensitive than ever.

Over the next few weeks, my heightened awareness of Dana's issues led me to conclude that her condition was worsening. She continued to have memory lapses. By this time I was becoming less and less comfortable letting Dana leave the house alone and made every attempt to limit her going solo. Whether or not I was with her, each time she left the house, she would check to see that everything she might need was in her purse—her cellphone, her wallet, and her many lists of things she didn't want to forget. Once in the car she would panic and go back inside to check again. I watched her compile endless lists. She made one, then another, then possibly not transfer an item from one list to another, compounding her conviction that the task had not been completed.

She often complained of dizziness, comparing the sensation to being on a boat. She said the sensation was worst first thing in the morning, and she would sit on the edge of the bed to get her bearings before standing up. Her dizziness seemed to get worse if she turned her head quickly.

The day came for Dana to undergo the comprehensive neurological examination at the Midwest Medical Center. They informed us it would take up a large part of the day. She was not looking forward to it. She was resistant to the idea of even doing it. Her dislike of going to doctors was increasing. That was certainly exacerbated by the frustration she was experiencing and the doubts she was having about what was going on in her mind. Fear, doubt, and paranoia made going to this appointment stressful for someone the doctors didn't want placed in stressful situations.

We showed up at the appointed time and place and met the neuropsychologist who was going to conduct the evaluation along with his assistant. His office was down a dark and dingy hallway, was claustrophobic, and looked very much like something out of *One Flew Over the Cuckoo's Nest*. I met with them for a short time, and then he asked me to leave so they could begin Dana's evaluation. The doctor said it would be several hours, they would break for lunch, and they would call me when Dana was ready to go. I left the medical center and went home with nothing really planned for the remainder of the day. That was about 9:00 in the morning.

It was almost 10:30 a.m. when my phone rang and the psychologist's assistant asked me to return to the medical center as soon as I could. Dana was not doing well, and they could not get her to do anything. They needed me to come and try to calm her down. It didn't take me very long to get back to the Medical Center. I went directly to the area where I had left Dana to find her sitting in the dark, dingy hallway on a wooden bench with her head in her hands, sobbing. Shockingly, she was completely alone. No one was in sight.

THIS CAN NEVER, EVER HAPPEN! The worst word in medical care is ALONE! Before you leave, make sure that the people whose JOB IT IS to CARE for your loved one understand that THEY ARE NOT TO BE LEFT ALONE FOR A MOMENT. EVER. There is an element of physical abandonment of care here because all medical and nursing care providers understand that they have a clear and continuing legal obligation to meet the physical and emotional needs of patients entrusted to their care. It's patently obvious that leaving a distraught Alzheimer's patient to suffer

and sob alone in an empty hallway is cruel at the very least and po-
tentially criminal had any actual harm taken place. Do I make myself
absolutely clear? Good. Make sure you do too. Accept no excuses.

When Dana saw me she stood up, grabbed me, and begged me
not to leave her and to take her home. She was distraught, simul-
taneously talking and sobbing, telling me, "That awful doctor kept
drilling me with questions I can't answer." She said he kept drilling
her and drilling her and wouldn't stop.

I tried my best to calm and comfort her. After about fifteen minutes, the doctor's assistant came out and tried to reason with Dana.
The assistant told me that the doctor hoped to resume the evaluation. That wasn't the message Dana wanted to hear, but after visiting with her a little while longer, I convinced Dana it was in
her—and our—best interest to give it another try. She reluctantly
agreed after I promised to stay at the medical center while she continued with the evaluation.

I went to a waiting area furnished with two wooden benches—
it resembled a bus or train station from the 1940s—and settled
down, expecting to be there for several more hours. A short time
later the assistant came out with a sobbing, agitated, and distraught Dana saying she couldn't stand it anymore. The assistant
said the doctor agreed that the examination should be suspended.

Furious and upset, I asked to speak with the doctor. Our conversation was very short and less than cordial. I told him, among
other things, that he might consider a future with the CIA special-
izing in enhanced interrogation procedures. He admitted that his
engagement with Dana had caused her great anxiety and emotional
distress and that the evaluation ended in a "nearly catastrophic
testing situation".

Catastrophic? Hell, it was barbaric.

He thought her cognitive difficulty was due to some underlying
neurological dysfunction.

You think?

Other than that, his report to Dana's neurologist and our family doctor was essentially worthless.

As you might imagine, after this experience I had great difficulty persuading Dana to return to the Medical Center for an MRI. Suffice it say, she did not want to go and told me in no uncertain terms that she was "sick and tired of being prodded and poked." Notwithstanding, we got through the MRI process relatively unscathed, but not totally without issues resulting from Dana's now full-blown doctor phobia.

We managed to avoid doctors for several weeks until we went back to Midwest Med for Dana's follow-up exam. It had now been some three or four months since the initial visit. Everything from then to now—Dana's behavior, the visit with the psychiatrist, the disaster with the neuropsychiatrist, and the MRI—were discussed with Dr. Weller. I told her that Dana's headaches and dizziness had worsened significantly after the neuropsychological testing episode disaster.

After we had been with Dr. Weller for a couple of hours or so, she brought up the possibility that Dana may have Alzheimer's disease but that it was very early and was probably being complicated by anxiety. Throughout the long series of tests and medical appointments, we had assembled a list of possible causes for Dana's deteriorating condition. They ranged from a brain tumor to some kind of circulatory disturbance to complex migraine—and yes, even to the possibility of some kind of dementia or Alzheimer's disease. That said, to hear the formal diagnosis of Alzheimer's disease, even with room for some diagnostic uncertainty, was shocking beyond words. All of the oxygen seemed to rush out of my lungs, and I wasn't sure where my next thought would take me. Remarkably, Dana received the devastating news with apparent calm. I can only guess that she did not understand the significance or the consequences of what had been said.

I was stunned. Who wouldn't be floored and anxious after what she had been going through? From alcohol to Alzheimer's? Give me a break! It was a bumpy trip from alcohol to Alzheimer's through the Midwest Medical Center. With the sole exception of Dr. Weller, it was depressing, unsatisfying, and they were completely insensitive and sometimes barbaric. They really made a meal of it. I don't even remember the drive home.

Another gentle reminder on a point of vital importance here. If you find yourself in serious emotional distress, where you feel like your loved one has been treated with a lack of sensitivity, a cavalier or patronizing attitude, or if you are not confident in the skill and competence of your medical professionals, you should seriously consider making a change. You may not be hopeful about the situation in which you find yourself, but you must have unwavering confidence in the people who are supposed to know how best to help you, especially if they do this for a living!

When I got my wits about me, I went to see Dr. Monaco and told him that I felt very strongly that I should take Dana to a medical center of excellence. I hoped it was not Alzheimer's and that we would find something less ominous and treatable. Since we had a home in Scottsdale, it was only natural that we could go there and go to the Mayo Clinic. Dr. Monaco arranged for an appointment at Mayo's neurology department, and we were off on the next step of the journey.

We were looking forward to going to Mayo. That was the first doctor visit in a long time where she was relatively eager to go. Our experience at the Midwest Medical Center left me skeptical, but I was still hopeful. We both were well aware of the Mayo Clinic's reputation, and while we didn't know anything about the doctor we were going to see, we both expected and anticipated that the experience would be an improvement over the chamber of horrors from which we just emerged. We also hoped and prayed that the diagnosis would change.

While we chose to go to the Mayo Clinic, it wasn't a slam dunk decision. It had the practical advantage that we owned a home nearby, but on the recommendation of some physician friends of mine, I had also investigated the possibility of taking Dana to Johns Hopkins, which was highly regarded in the diagnosis and treatment of dementia. My research led me to believe that while excellent, they were no better than the Mayo Clinic, so convenience and comfort tipped the scale in the decision. As with most medical centers of excellence, you don't just make an appointment to see the doctor next Tuesday. Mayo would first need all of Dana's records, have a chance to review them, assign the appropriate professionals, and then have scheduling contact us. The process to get the first appointment took several weeks.

Chapter 4:
The Last Day of the First Part of Our Lives

We arrived at the Mayo Clinic. We found the place to be bright, cheery, and spotless. Starting with checking in on that first day, I found Mayo to be extremely efficient and patient-centered. They went out of their way to make sure that the patient and the patient's family were fully informed at all times, were reassured, and were comfortable every step of the way. The check-in process was smooth, and although it was a major medical center of excellence, you never felt lost or unsure of what to do or where to go next. That was our first of what would become dozens of appointments to come at Mayo.

We checked in and took a seat in a warm, bright, and cheerful reception area. Our appointment was scheduled at 8:00 a.m. When Dana's name was called, I looked down at my watch, and it was 8:00 a.m., which we came to find out was standard for Mayo. It's a rare Mayo happening if anyone ever has to wait beyond their appointment time.

We were greeted by a nurse who took Dana's arm in a very soft and gentle way. She led her down a very bright, wide, well-lit, and nicely appointed hallway, then asked if she would step on a scale to take her height and weight measurements. The nurse was disarmingly charming with Dana, telling her that nobody liked to step on those scales. She jokingly told Dana that she would fudge it as best she could. We were then led into an examination room that was spotless, spacious, and very pleasantly appointed. The nurse took Dana's temperature, blood pressure, pulse, and blood oximetry. She then said that the doctor would be with us momentarily and left the room.

Fourteen seconds later (exaggeration to make a point), there was a little rap on the door, and Dr. Richard Caselli came into the room and introduced himself. Tall and slim with glasses and dark hair, he was a very gentle, soft-spoken, professorial-looking man with a broad, relaxed smile. Over his crisp business shirt and tie, he wore a houndstooth-style sports coat that could have been worn by his father at some time, and a pair of well-worn shoes that looked designed more for comfort than for fashion. He had a slight stoop that made it seem like he was reaching down to you, and his handshake was somehow comforting and calming. He listened carefully and spoke kindly, maintaining constant eye contact and thoughtful attention as we talked. Most importantly, he made us feel very comfortable from the moment he entered the room.

Pay attention to how the experts make you FEEL. They may have the most brilliant minds in the history of medicine, but if they lack empathy and compassion, they are worse than useless to you. This is one situation in which you need—and deserve—the whole package: a well-rounded, caring person who can help you and truly care for you, particularly when there is the possibility of bad news. If you don't feel absolutely comfortable and feel you are in the very best hands, go elsewhere!

He had clearly done his homework and could discuss minute details of everything that had been done to Dana during the visits to our family physician, the psychiatrist, and the Midwest Medical Center. He was soft, he was gentle, and he was very non-threatening. He did the standard exam that Dana had now done several times, checking her reflexes, gait stability, and vision tracking.

When Dr. Caselli told Dana he was going ask her a few questions, she immediately stiffened and got the tightened upper lip look that occurred each time she was about to confront the MMSE. She told Dr. Caselli she wasn't happy being forced to answer questions she had difficulty answering, and she didn't want to answer the questions. I can only tell you that Dr. Caselli then conducted the MMSE evaluation almost without Dana knowing that it was happening. The guy had a gift.

The good news was that the experience was a non-event emotionally for Dana. The bad news is that she scored worse on the test than the last time she had taken it. Dr. Caselli was clear and candid in his discussion with us, yet soft and gentle enough that Dana was no more alarmed in discussing her condition than she had been before seeing him. He told us that after reviewing her record and from the brief examination he had just conducted, that there was a distinct possibility that she might have some cognitive issues. But he was unwilling to label her condition until we had the opportunity to explore everything that could possibly result in the loss of cognitive ability, from brain cancer to Valley Fever. He told us that with our patience and cooperation, we would find out what was at the root of Dana's condition. I believed him.

So, the Mayo Clinic journey began.

We spent the next several months eliminating possible suspects, while the Mayo Clinic under Dr. Caselli's direction vigorously and competently treated her symptoms. Each time a possible reason for her condition was eliminated, I grew more worried that indeed Dana may be suffering from Alzheimer's. As Mayo was exploring the far reaches of her brain, I remember wishing they would find a brain tumor they'd be able to operate on and treat rather than leave us with no hope at all.

Dana was sent to psychiatrists to help her cope with anxiety and potential depression, although I think her anxiety about her condition far outweighed any depression she may have been suffering. They gave her exercises, and games, and thought processes to work on to help her relax and contend with her difficulties. She was referred to the Mayo Pain Clinic to help manage her headaches, which became increasingly severe. They ran test after test, study after study, performed electroencephalographs, sent her to the sleep clinic, tested her spinal fluid pressure, and did spinal taps for laboratory studies while they medicated her symptoms. Dr. Caselli showed a great deal of interest in the anxiety or panic attacks that Dana experienced from time to time. While she hadn't had a severe one for a couple of months, he continued to be concerned about them. He discussed with me the possibility they were seizure-like and what might be causing them.

He was also interested in a tremor Dana had in her right hand. She'd had it for many years, but it had worsened noticeably in the last three or four years. He tried several medications to relieve the tremor and at one point thought it might be indicative of Lewy body dementia, which is accompanied by Parkinson's-like symptoms. After extensive study and evaluation, he eliminated that possibility.

Dr. Caselli also sent Dana for an all-day neuropsychological evaluation like her catastrophic experience at the Midwest Medical Center. Since I was not in attendance, I don't know how they managed or what magic they performed, but they were able to complete the evaluation without the emotional, gut-wrenching reaction she suffered in her previous encounter with this evaluation. This time when Dana was finished, she even came out with the doctor who administered the test with a smile on her face.

The clinic performed exhaustive studies eliminating both common and rare viruses that might have affected Dana neurologically, including Valley Fever since we spent time in the Arizona desert.

From my perspective, it seemed like they did every conceivable scan of her head and brain, all of which proved to be essentially negative. In summary, they turned Dana upside down, inside out, and every way but loose, and after several months of prodding and probing, testing and retesting, examining and scanning, they arrived at the dreaded conclusion that the only thing they were unable to eliminate was Alzheimer's-like dementia.

When Dr. Caselli finally uttered the words I dreaded hearing, he took me aside and sat down with me to talk about where, in his opinion, Dana was in the progression of her disease. He carefully and painstakingly described what was going to happen to her over time and what I was about to experience as her caregiver. He did this with grace and compassion. He also asked me if Dana was receiving Social Security disability, a thought that had never entered my mind. He said that she qualified, and I would be well served to get the process started as soon as possible. His words rang in my ears and should ring in the ears of every family that faces this dreaded diagnosis.

He said, "Dick, this will be a long, long, painful and very expensive experience. You will need all the help you can get."

You work all your life paying Social Security taxes, in the hope of receiving those benefits in retirement. Do not, I repeat, do NOT forget that Social Security benefits are also available for disabilities, and there can be no disability more punishing or potentially long-lasting than Alzheimer's—particularly with early onset Alzheimer's. The cost of care is unbelievable, and regardless of your circumstances, disability benefits will ease the financial burden. Apply for Social Security disability benefits as soon as the diagnosis is made, and brace yourself for the pain of dealing with the process and the bureaucrats.

I couldn't tell exactly how Dana felt. She was quiet and tearful but seemed resolved and relatively steady. I didn't know then, and I will never know, if she totally comprehended what she had just heard. I walked away feeling that this was now the last day of the first part of our lives, and I was resolute that I would take care of Dana in the manner I would want her to take care of me—in style and grace—for as long as I was physically and financially able. That was my promise to her.

We spent the next few weeks in Scottsdale trying to enjoy our home away from home, being out in the fresh air and sunshine, although Dana didn't like going on the long walks we used to enjoy so much. Over the previous couple of years, our walks had become shorter and shorter. I still tried to get her to go for walks with me, knowing it would be good for both of us to be out and getting some exercise. It was also a time for Dana to decompress from the barrage of doctors and medical, psychological, cognitive, and neurological testing she had undergone over the last several months. We knew we had to get back to Kansas, but for a time we were in no hurry to do so. It was the first part of the last of Dana's life.

Chapter 5:
The Best Things in Life are Not Things

In time we started thinking about going back home and taking a look at the world from the Midwest. Once back in Kansas my mind went into overdrive trying to comprehend what life was going to be like from now on. We had a beautiful home in Leawood, one that Dana and I had designed and built just on the cusp of her starting to go through menopause. We both loved the house and everything about it, from Dana's Steinway and our huge outdoor fireplace to my wine cellar next to the steam room. It was the home we had always dreamed of, and in many ways it was comfortable settling back into the Midwest frame of mind, at least in the short term.

As the weeks went by Dana's condition didn't seem to be deteriorating fast, but she certainly wasn't getting any better. It was still a struggle trying to get things straight; there was still anxiety when she lost an item or couldn't remember something. She was a little bit more irascible with each passing week, and I was slowly learning to become more accommodating each time her irritability and hostility increased. Clearly, she had been dealt an incredibly bad hand, but I was determined to help her play that hand the best that we could.

As the weather started turning colder, and we were shut in a little bit more, I thought we ought to grab a plane for Scottsdale to thaw out and get some sun. Plus, Dana was struggling with the size and complexities of our home in Kansas City. Just the facilities made it a more complicated home to manage than our condo in Scottsdale, where Dana seemed more at ease. The pattern of alternating between a few weeks in Scottsdale and a few weeks in Kansas City continued for the next several months, with the time spent in Scottsdale increasing and the time spent in Kansas City decreasing.

In Kansas City, Dana was a real handful. She couldn't run the washer or dryer because it wasn't like the one in Arizona. She couldn't operate the appliances or work the shower because they weren't like the ones in Scottsdale. It became clear that her mind could get around our little condo in Scottsdale but just couldn't expand to comfortably negotiate the house in Kansas City.

It became more difficult to tell what Dana was thinking or what was going through her mind. It was also becoming increasingly difficult to discuss our living pattern rationally with her. In my mind it was clear that she would be unable to tolerate living in two different homes, and I would be unable to manage her if I tried to force it. Her mind had shrunk to where the condo was the right fit. When adding in that she loved the weather in Scottsdale, it became clear to me that we should sell the home in Kansas City that we loved so dearly. It had become a thing, and things were becoming less and less important every day.

I remember broaching this idea with Dana, thinking that I would meet quite a bit of resistance. To the contrary, she thought that our moving primarily to Scottsdale was the right thing to do. To this day I don't know how she came to that conclusion. I'm sure it wasn't from the perspective that her diminished cognitive abilities made it difficult for her to manage living in two places. I think it was the promise created by the mindset that we loved escaping to the Valley of the Sun, and life had always been lighter and less stressful and more fun when we were in Arizona. But wherever we lived, life no longer held the promise it once did for Dana, and never would again. My life had changed forever as well.

So the decision was made. We would sell our Kansas home and make the Valley of the Sun our primary residence. We'd keep a smaller place in the Kansas City area to maintain our Kansas residency. I wasn't looking forward to selling a house that was built right before the real estate bubble and before the value of real estate had a chance to recover, but sell the house we did, at a considerable loss I might add. We hastily rented a condo in Leawood to be our Kansas home.

It was bad enough managing Dana through her ups and downs, her quirks and eccentricities, her agitation and anxieties, and her panic attacks and increasingly hostile moods, which were becoming more acute every day. Adding the experiences of selling a 5,000-square-foot house and moving into a 1,600-square-foot condo and uprooting thirty years of history in the Midwest and transplanting it to the desert Southwest, I was near the breaking point. I would have either not made the move or might have quit right in the middle of it had not every one of Dana's doctors agreed that the move would be the best thing for her.

It was now time to start making choices that neither of us had ever thought about making. The really difficult part about making these choices was that Dana was no longer able to be rational, reasonable, or thoughtful. I never knew what her reaction might be when presented with a set of facts or even a simple question. But it didn't matter what her reaction was when first presented with the opportunity to make a decision because once the decision was made it could very likely change five days later or five hours later or even five minutes later. Her hostility and unreasonableness increased whenever I tried to get her input about something we were doing. She was particularly hostile when something was being done she had initially agreed to but then later changed her mind about or didn't remember having agreed to it in the first place. We struggled and agonized over decision after decision after decision. Little things became monumental; big things trivial. There was no way to anticipate what was going to be around the next corner.

Her prized Steinway went to our great friends Chuck and Jennifer Laue. Dana was a little tearful but was happy it would be in such a wonderful home with friends she loved so dearly. I know that somewhere in the back of her mind she understood that her impairment would never again allow her to enjoy the instrument the way she knew it could and should be enjoyed.

But, for the most part, she just couldn't decide where this painting should go or that artifact could go or whether to keep an item or let it go. The whole idea of selling a big house and downsizing your possessions is stressful enough for the strongest. Can you only imagine how difficult it was for someone to live through this process while cognitively impaired? What should have taken two hours would take two days, and what should have taken two days took two weeks.

The agony of this undertaking was monumental. I'd pack boxes, and Dana would unpack them. Things would be set aside with no rhyme or reason to either go or stay, only for me to find out later that what went should have stayed and what stayed was no longer wanted. Items that were once important were no longer important, and it turned out that very few things carried any meaning to her at all. Then later I learned that might not have been the case.

Somehow we made it to the move. We furnished our 1,600-square-foot condo and put the remainder of our belongings that we were keeping—which was significant—into storage. We closed on the house and moved into the condo.

In the middle of this entire process, from the time that we first started talking about selling our home until the day we moved into our little condo in Leawood, I visited with Dana's doctor about her deteriorating condition and lack of interest in anything going on around her. He suggested I consider getting Dana a puppy. He thought it would help calm and soothe her and give her something to be interested in.

So, by God, I got her a puppy!

Boomer, a rescue from the animal shelter, was going to be part of the family. Clearly, we wouldn't be able to deal with an unruly, untrained puppy, so Boomer was sent to live with a trainer for a couple of months. When he came home from finishing school, he was a bright, snappy, trained puppy and was the most delightful animal anyone could ever hope to have in their home—and continues to be to this day.

Boomer was the most appealing little scrap of fluffy fur you could imagine. He was mostly white, with a couple of black spots on his back and tummy. He had soft, droopy black and white ears and quizzical, soft brown eyes with a tail that wagged constantly. He was, to put it kindly, a puppy of uncertain parentage; the best guess the rescue staff could give us was a terrier/poodle mix because his soft coat did not shed. He was extremely intelligent and had the disarming habit of tilting his head to the left if you asked him a question. With a tennis ball in your hand, Boomer would do your calculus homework for you. His natural posture was relaxed, to say the least; if he sat for any length of time, he slouched over giving the impression that he was perched on one of his haunches, rather than sitting up straight. He was completely scruffy and almost impossibly cute and grew up to weigh about twenty-five pounds.

Dana loved Boomer, and Boomer loved Dana. But it was all I could do to keep Boomer trained because Dana was unable to be consistent with him or remember his commands. Nonetheless, except for her ruining his ability to walk properly on a leash, Boomer and the two of us got along famously. But someday I'll have to visit with Dana's doctor again about his advice to get a puppy. Dana lost interest in Boomer, although she enjoyed having him around, and Boomer became an additional responsibility for me - one I didn't need. Suffice it to say that Boomer and I are still together. We are great friends, and he has helped me through all the challenges and heartache we experienced going through our tragedy.

We stayed in the Leawood condo for a short time. Dana was not comfortable or happy in the new, unfamiliar condo, and with each passing day I became increasingly smothered by the closeness of the condo and the cloud over Dana's head. That was not how I had envisioned us enjoying our retirement years although since learning of Dana's diagnosis, enjoying life and looking forward to those things we had always planned had taken a back seat.

I reached the point where relief was needed, so we packed Boomer in the car and pointed it towards Scottsdale.

Chapter 6:
Today is Better Than Tomorrow

By now you might have the impression that there were a number of trips between Kansas City and Phoenix. Indeed, there were. For someone who is cognitively challenged and whose abilities are diminishing with each passing day, travel becomes a real adventure. Dana and I traveled a lot when we were still working, but the travel was limited to leisure and vacation time. We had been looking forward to traveling more extensively when we didn't have the demands of the real world holding us back.

But in our new world, every trip with Dana became more and more cumbersome and more and more difficult. She couldn't pack her own suitcase and if she tried would never pack all the things she needed. If I packed for her, she'd come along later and unpack to see what was in the suitcase and get furious with me if something wasn't in there she thought should be. When I worked with her to include those different things, I'd discover an hour or so later that once again she had unpacked the suitcase. It was a circus trying to get her organized to go anywhere.

You can imagine the bewildering battle waged trying to pack her cosmetics. It happened whether we were driving or flying, and getting

Dana through security in an airport, particularly if she had to go through an X-ray machine or body search, was a nightmare. When we drove, getting her in and out of a hotel, trying to convince her to sleep in a strange bed, and trying to explain where we were and where we were going was a continual and painful process.

Except for one trip back to Leawood for a few days during the holidays, Dana had seen the Leawood condo for the last time. It was too strange, too impersonal, too... I don't know what, but she couldn't stay there, and I had no compelling reason to try to force it except that we remained legal residents of Kansas. We had moved from a large house into a small condo and spent very few days and nights in it. Going forward, Scottsdale would be home base for Dana and me and Boomer, of course.

It was on that last trip to Kansas that we applied for Social Security disability for Dana. The process is intrusive and cumbersome, as are most things with the government. I dreaded the process, but Dr. Caselli's words that the course of Dana's disease would be *long and VERY expensive* continued to resonate. She had worked all her life and paid Social Security taxes. It's reasonable to expect the benefits you're entitled to. Once qualified, she would receive full Social Security benefits as though she had reached retirement age, even though she was still several years away. Age doesn't matter in disability cases.

After the government had received the paperwork, we were notified that Dana had to be interviewed by a social worker to determine her eligibility. Far be it for the United States government to believe the word of an esteemed Mayo Clinic neurologist that Dana was disabled. They had to see it for themselves, and that's where it went from bad to worse. The social worker informed us that Dana would have to undergo a complete neurological evaluation along with extensive cognitive testing conducted by a government psychologist.

You gotta be kidding, right? Right? Two, not one, but two medical centers had already said Dana was disabled. But no, they weren't kidding! The government needed proof that up was up and down was down. Take your multivitamins—and your antacids—grit your teeth, and brace yourself. The government is here to help. RIGHT? Only after they exhaust every other avenue. And you.

The day came for the testing. I knew the only way I could get her there was to lie about where we were going. Suffice it to say, even in her diminished capacity, she understood enough to become completely unstitched. In time, I got her calmed down enough to begin the process. The government psychologist was several notches below the Midwest Medical Center's doctor who was such a disaster. By the time the psychologist completed what testing could be done under the circumstances, Dana was a sobbing, shaking mass of protoplasm. The process was cruel and inhumane, shocking and sad, and completely unnecessary. Upon completion, the psychologist pronounced that Dana was cognitively impaired and mentally disabled. You think? Our government at work...

I have always said—and will probably repeat it several times to emphasize the point—the one constant about Alzheimer's disease is that you can be sure tomorrow will always be worse than today. There is nothing to look forward to. Today is as good as it's going to get. One other thing you should know about coping as a caregiver and managing the Alzheimer's patient is that you never know what's around the next corner. Just when you say things couldn't get any worse, and you're convinced that they can't get any worse, they do.

Dana was occupying all my time, my mindshare, and my emotions. But I decided to take the time to have my annual physical—sort of like putting on your own oxygen mask first. It was fortunate I didn't postpone or cancel that visit because I was diagnosed with prostate cancer.

No, this wasn't made up by a team of bad Hollywood scriptwriters. This was REALLY HAPPENING, even though it should have been in a B-grade horror movie. And that's the lesson here—your life does not stop when you become immersed in the world of Alzheimer's. Stuff happens, and most of it feels like bad stuff. There's always the possibility of some other weird shoe dropping right on your head, and it always seems to happen when you least expect it and when you feel like you can least deal with it.

That was all we needed. I didn't tell Dana about it for some time, and when I did tell her, she greeted the news with relative indifference, a response that only validated the seriousness of her cognitive decline. That was not my Dana. So, not only did I want to get Dana out of Kansas City for all the reasons previously stated, but I also had scheduled an appointment at the Mayo Clinic for a prostate cancer workup.

I include the prostate cancer intrusion not for sympathy for me, but to illustrate that life does not stop or even slow down in the face of dealing with Alzheimer's. Dana's condition could not be put on hold for me to deal with my problem. I couldn't choose to set aside caring for and looking after her until there was some resolution to the disease I faced. Looking after Dana had become a 24/7/365 job. I couldn't go to the doctor and leave her home alone. As my medical visits increased so did the pressure from her deteriorating condition. I'd take her along to the Mayo Clinic and make sure someone at check-in would keep an eye on her while I was in with the doctors. She couldn't—or wouldn't—understand why we had to go to the doctor so much, but at least it wasn't the battle it would have been had we been going for her. And then there was Boomer. His kennel with treats and an occasional look-in by a neighbor helped a lot.

After consulting with my doctors, we decided that my best treatment option was to have surgery as opposed to radiation and/or chemo. How to have surgery with the subsequent recovery and look after Dana at the same time was going to be a challenge. The surgery option also had the advantage of fewer trips to the doctor than the other treatments required—assuming the surgery proved successful.

I hoped Dawn would be the answer to help me get through this. Dawn is my daughter, and for the last couple of years or so she had come to visit from Denver to give me a break here and there from the constant and continual vigilance of caring for Dana. We decided that the surgery would be scheduled when Dawn could come to Scottsdale. Dawn is my daughter, not Dana's, but they were as close as any devoted mother and daughter could be. They shared remarkable qualities, including the uncanny ability to appreciate people with loving hearts and sincere characters. Their relationship was important to each of them and was wonderful for me to watch over the years.

Dawn arrived. She and Dana drove me to the hospital for surgery and sat with me for the time allowed pre-op. Dana was pretty much detached as we made small talk and passed the time. She didn't seem able to comprehend the situation but seemed content that it was not her being poked and prodded. As Dana got more and more removed, we decided that she and Dawn would go home and return when I was out of recovery. That would be better for everyone as Dawn would have her hands full taking care of Dana and watching after Boomer. Dana had become increasingly demanding about things like eating and comfort for herself and less tolerant about any delayed satisfaction or gratification.

I went to surgery; the next thing I knew I was waking up—some five hours later. Dawn was holding my hand while Dana was sitting in the corner of my hospital room looking out the window. Recovery in the hospital, while painful and uncomfortable, was uneventful. I was home in a couple of days and found that Dawn had managed to keep Dana safe and marginally happy in my absence; however,

Dawn was frazzled and at the tipping point. That was Dawn's first experience of the 24/7 nature of taking care of Dana, and she will tell you that she had no idea the toll it took to be on call, on edge, and on alert all day and all night.

The next couple of days were consumed with me trying to recover and Dawn playing nursemaid to me while also taking care of Dana (and Boomer). Picture my poor daughter trying to satisfy Dana's incessant demands and needs while at the same time helping me adjust my catheter. What a trooper and lovely, sensitive, loyal and committed daughter I am blessed to have. She is a saint. Dawn stayed for a couple of more days and then had to return to Denver.

I resumed the lonely duty of caring for Dana notwithstanding my ongoing post-surgery recovery. In many respects, Dana's condition helped me through my recovery. It didn't give me time to feel sorry for myself or wallow in self-pity. I had a solemn responsibility and committed duty to take care of her, and nothing would keep me from doing so, and there was simply no time and little energy left for anything else. Alzheimer's disease, like rust, never sleeps.

As the days turned into weeks and the weeks turned into months that all melted together, Dana's condition continued to worsen. It was getting ever more difficult to manage the eccentricities caused by the loss of her cognitive abilities. I tried to get her out of the house as much as possible. We went to breakfast, an activity we had always enjoyed. In the past, I used to work at breakfast and read the newspapers. Dana would do Sudoku puzzles. Now, however, Sudoku was out of the picture, and the time was consumed with me trying to anticipate how to occupy or deflect Dana's attention.

Ordering food became a burden because Dana could no longer navigate a menu. Choices overwhelmed her. Knowing from experience what she usually ordered, I suggested some alternatives she might like and systematically narrowed the choices until we got to a couple she could pick from. Invariably when breakfast was served it wasn't "what I ordered." We would either reorder, or I would trade with her, having learned to order one of her alternatives for myself in the likelihood she would reject what she was served. Whatever she ended up with would often be too hot or too cold, too salty or too sweet, or whatever else a demented mind might imagine about what it sees or tastes.

Eating breakfast out was becoming a burden I could do without. So, from going out to breakfast five or six times a week, we started going two or three times a week and ultimately reduced the number to an occasional breakfast out. I missed getting out of the house in the morning and greeting the world over a bought cup of coffee, but was not unhappy avoiding the confrontations and scenes made by the turmoil caused over breakfast. The alternative was for me to cook/prepare/assemble breakfast or go to the market and pick up something. I always had to get several choices to satisfy Dana's flawed decision-making abilities, and even then most mornings were greeted with complaints and dissatisfaction.

The freedom of choice, or choices in general, are serious problems for people with Alzheimer's. Daily living is hard enough, but making choices becomes impossible. The collapse of decision-making is part of the disease process; do whatever you can to navigate your way through the swamp.

Obviously, Dana and Boomer would accompany me to the market to get breakfast. In the main I could convince her to stay in the car with Boomer while I ran into the store. And I could usually park the car in a place where I could keep an eye on it.

Dana had long since stopped driving. One of the top decisions that must be made when dealing with an Alzheimer's patient is when to take away the keys to the car—and to make sure they can't find them! I understand the automobile represents an Alzheimer's victim's last rays of freedom and independence, but early on, their ability to timely filter through all the stimuli hitting their brain while driving is so diminished that operating an automobile is just out of the question. Taking away the keys elicited the most hostility from Dana toward me, not only at the time but for many months after. Unprovoked, Dana would fly into a rage on an almost daily basis, attacking me for not letting her drive. For some reason Alzheimer's disease doesn't seem to affect the memory as it relates to losing one's driving privileges as early as it does for other things. Over the months and years, of all the things that Dana could no longer re-member—both near and far—she always knew that I kept her from driving, and she never let me forget it in the harshest and some-times crudest ways. Researchers might want to study this phenom-enon in their search for the clues to Alzheimer's disease.

While going out to dinner had similar results, I think it was more painful in some respects. Again, I'll never know if Dana had any feelings about our changing life and circumstances. We loved going out to dinner. It had always been our time. A time when we reflected on the day, the week, the season. A time when we planned, and we dreamed. It was a time when we relaxed and visited, some-times about serious subjects but often about nothing in particular.

Dana loved a cosmopolitan before dinner. I preferred a lemon drop martini. We both would have a glass of wine with our entrée. Dana a white wine, me a good wine. As you might expect by now, the scourge of Alzheimer's invaded and destroyed this special space of ours. Either the cosmopolitan was too sour or too sweet. Dana could not choose a wine. The restaurant was too hot or too cool. The restaurant was too dark. It was too loud. The air conditioning was blowing on her, and we had to move. The seating was too close to the kitchen. The food was too hot or too cold. *That isn't what I ordered.* The steak was over-done or too rare. The fish tasted fishy. On and on...

I would send her dinner back for another, or I would exchange mine for hers and end up eating something I didn't order and didn't like. That's all in the job. She got so sensitive that she would not eat her filet, her favorite steak, because it had grill marks on it. She would ask: *What is that; what are those stripes?* When told they were grill marks from cooking the steak on the grill, she either couldn't understand or wouldn't understand and refused to eat it.

The scene and disruption were uncomfortable, and I'm sure the restaurant staff and other patrons didn't appreciate the commotion. Dana had lost her ability to realize that she was making a scene. She would become loud and obnoxious—all this coming from the sweetest, softest, most gentle, and considerate person I had ever known. Like breakfast, where we once would go out for dinner four or five times a week, I was forced to limit it to once or twice and then just occasionally. Eventually, dinner out became a thing of the past.

I'm not going to tell you not to take the person you're caring for out in public, but you need to know that it will become increasingly difficult to navigate through social norms and social settings. You'll know it when you see it, and you will need to adjust accordingly.

Where we once went to movies often, I could no longer take her. She couldn't follow the storyline or even recognize the characters from scene to scene. The more questions she had, the more frustrated she got—and the louder she got. Going to the movies was history.

While not big television fans in the past, we watched it occasionally. I always liked sporting events and a little news. But as with movies she now couldn't follow an episode or a sporting event and was bothered that I was watching and she wasn't. She would sit and complain. She didn't like the noise. It was causing her a headache. Nothing, it seemed, could satisfy her, please her, or bring her any enjoyment.

As her disease progressed, her sensitivities shifted into high alert. Temperature became exaggerated and extreme. The bedroom was too hot or too cold. The water was boiling or freezing. There was no way to appease her environmental sensitivities. Turn the air conditioning down and it got too cold. Turn it back up and it got too hot. Mind you, this was not occasionally. The trips to the thermostat were constant, often to change what she had done because she could no longer discern one button from another. I had to be vigilant all day, every day, to the possibility/probability that she would change settings on everything from the thermostat to the refrigerator, stovetop range, or anything else that had a knob, button, or control panel.

Where once Dana had read a lot, she could no longer read. It went from not being able to remember from chapter to chapter, to not remembering from page to page, to not being able to track the words in a sentence. Magazines were out as well. She even lost interest in looking at the pictures.

Dana had always loved to go shopping. As you can imagine, shopping trips deteriorated into disasters. Where once she loved to buy shoes, she could no longer make choices. She lost interest in shoes, clothes, and shopping altogether. The only shopping trips were for absolute necessities. A great example—bras. Buying a brassiere was a real pain. The only thing I knew about bras I learned as a teenager—how to unhook them with one hand. Now circumstances forced me to help make decisions about fit and support from the hundreds of choices available. While doing this, Dana was yelling and cursing through her frustration, long after she chased the sales clerk—and fitting expert—out of the dressing room.

You're going to need to do things that you never imagined you would need to do. For me it was shopping for lingerie and cosmetics. Summon as much dignity and calm as you can, but be prepared to abandon the expedition if it goes totally off the rails. The objective is always live to fight another day, but don't procrastinate too much because today is always better than tomorrow.

Once a beautifully made-up, put together, and dressed woman, Dana lost interest in both her clothes and looks. It was up to me to make sure she showered, washed her hair, brushed her teeth, put on makeup—and I had to fight her every step of the way. She either didn't want to do it or thought she had already done it and refused to do it again. We'll never know which, and it didn't matter. The result was the same, and she didn't care. The simplest things flared into screaming sessions and battles fought but never won. I learned to walk away and re-approach, deflect, distract, or just forget. I knew the last eruption would subside and the next battle or explosion was just around the corner and would erupt when least expected.

Dana's doctors prescribed a few drugs for her. Some were to calm her, some to help her with the tremor in her right hand, some to help "sharpen her mind" (Aricept, Namenda) and some regular health issue drugs (cholesterol) along with a few supplements. Some were prescribed once a day at different times. Some were prescribed multiple times a day. Clearly, she couldn't administer her own medication. So several times a day there were ugly—very ugly—confrontations surrounding the taking of medications. As with a shower, she claimed she had taken them or just refused to take them. She constantly wanted to know what she was taking and what it was for. From the time she was approached until the time she took the meds, I could spend hours cajoling, negotiating, distracting, deflecting, and lying. Yes, lying. Sadly, you have to learn to lie to manage an Alzheimer's patient. One does what needs to be done to get the medications down the hatch. If nothing else, it helped fill my day—-like there wasn't enough to do at this point.

On the subject of medications, it's my opinion that Alzheimer's medications are often prescribed more for the family and caregivers than the patient, so they'll believe that something is being done to help the patient. I could never discern any improvement from any drug prescribed for Dana. Doctors and researchers will readily admit that the effect of drugs commonly prescribed for Alzheimer's patients can be statistically measured in the laboratory but not necessarily in the behavior of the patient. Still, I prefer to follow a doctor's orders and administer the medications they prescribe.

Some neurologists describe the effects of Alzheimer's drugs, such as Aricept and Namenda, as being similar to going to consecutive football games in the Horseshoe at Ohio State University. The first game's attendance was 102,387 fans. The attendance at the next game was 101,842. If you were in the stands at both games, could you honestly say that you were able to tell the difference?

While fun-loving, Dana had always been polished and put together, reserved and measured, professional and classy. She wasn't flighty or reckless. She had now turned into the photo negative of herself. She was argumentative, combative, hostile, ill-tempered, sometimes uncontrollable—emotionally, not physically—verbally ugly and downright nasty, and would have been unclean and disheveled if it weren't for the continuing battles fought over her personal hygiene.

While she had always had a reserved nature, she now was totally uninhibited—or as my acquaintances from Missouri would say, uninhabited, which was probably also true—and said or did just about anything at any time. By any reasonable standards her language and actions were bizarre and crude and would have been embarrassing to her had she realized what she was doing or saying. She would have been mortified.

On one occasion she showed some acquaintances what she thought was a new dress she was wearing then pulled up her skirt to show them her old underwear. I learned to expect the unexpected at any time and in any place. Still, I was shocked whenever it happened. I just couldn't imagine the things that came out of Dana's mouth or the things she did and where she said or did them. I never got used to it but became numb to it.

Chapter 7:
One Step at a Time

Arizona was better than Kansas, but our condo in Scottsdale was beginning to be a problem, and I saw that it was going to become a bigger problem for me. While much nicer and somewhat larger than our Leawood condo, it was still too small. The master suite was upstairs. Downstairs had a kitchen, dining, and living area all in one large great room. Down a hallway were two guest bedrooms and a bath. Essentially, there was only one living area, and it was beginning to close in on me.

While I had to maintain constant vigilance on Dana's presence and activities, actually sitting in the same room all day, every day was driving me up a tree. Since very little seemed to satisfy her or make her happy, the hostilities, arguments, and confrontations that erupted were impossible to escape—-if only to another living space for a few minutes. I realized that I was going to require some relief, if only in physical space.

Secondly, it occurred to me that at some point I was going to need some help to take care of Dana. I had read and talked and thought a lot about that eventuality. My Mayo physician and Dana's doctors had all encouraged me to get extra help. They constantly reminded me that I would be no help if I literally killed myself trying to take care of her on my own.

Sounds so obvious, doesn't it??? You're not going to be able to do anything, much less help anyone—especially the one you care so much about—if you kill yourself in the process. And it's much easier to do than you'd think (the killing yourself part, folks) because you get immersed—or rather submerged—in the DOING of it and the COPING with it that you don't even notice that your own health is teetering on the edge. Your mental health is part of your overall health. Take a long, hard look at yourself, and take good care of yourself. Please.

After long thought and consideration and several hundred more in-your-face blowups over the most trivial issues, I considered buying a bigger house. I even looked at the longer run and thought about buying a house big enough to have live-in help if that should ever become a consideration or necessity. These mental gymnastics became a plan and then a reality. I bought a larger house for my peace of mind, Dana's comfort (I hoped), and any long-term care considerations. I was still resolute that Dana would live through her disease at home, that I would take care of her, and that I might get some part-time help from time to time—or more if absolutely necessary—to relieve some of the pressure.

On the positive side, I could move our things from storage in Kansas City to the new house, along with my wine collection, which I missed dearly. We could finally have all of what was left of our stuff in one place. Also, I thought it might help Dana to surround her with things she knew and loved and that were near and dear to her. Surely it would give her some warmth and comfort. But I came to realize that time had long since passed. If she remembered her things, she no longer cared. If she didn't remember them, it didn't matter anyway. Alzheimer's has a way of jamming absolute perspective down your throat. I kept being reminded that the best things in life are not things. There's no better teacher on this lesson than Alzheimer's disease.

Particularly sad was seeing Dana lose interest in the people she loved and the experiences she cherished. Sadness can't describe the anguish I experienced as the memory of people and life's moments faded from her once-vibrant personality. Dana's ability to light up a room was gone. This trait had been no more evident or pronounced than on birthdays—everyone's birthday. She single-handedly kept Hallmark cards in business when that dinosaur should have gone the way of computer punched data cards. Birthdays were very special to Dana, and everyone was special on their birthday. It was their day. Dana's birthday was no exception. In fact, it was the example. The celebration seemed endless. It wasn't in-your-face all for her. It was: *Come on everyone, let's celebrate.* She wanted to share her joy and happiness with everyone.

Appropriately, her birthday is the Fourth of July! She began the ramp up late in June, and the festivities would last through most of July. Everyone celebrated Dana's birthday. She made the folks feel good. It was a holiday, people had the day off, and fireworks were lit across the country celebrating Dana's birthday—oh, and the nation's birthday as well. Mint chocolate chip ice cream, white cake with white frosting, and watermelon—Dana's favorites—were in abundance, along with a couple of cosmopolitans.

My contribution to making her birthday special was to take her places that understood Independence Day/birthday celebrations. We went to Boston several times for fireworks on the Esplanade of the Charles River and to Washington, DC, to watch the fireworks over the Washington Monument from the Capitol steps. We went to New York for the Macy's fireworks display on the Hudson River, and to Chicago to celebrate the Fourth with fireworks at Navy Pier. Napa Valley was a favorite, watching several displays across the Valley from the terrace at Auberge du Soleil. These are probably my fondest memories of her alive, vibrant, happy life and the times we spent together. I'm heartbroken at the tragedy of her losing the memory of the precious moments of birthdays past, the experience of birthdays now, and the anticipation of birthdays yet to come. That is the scourge of Alzheimer's. It takes no prisoners. Everyone's birthdays are now gone including Dana's, and birthdays are now just like every other day—confusing, upsetting, turbulent, combative, hostile, and fearful.

So, we moved to our new home. Dana, Boomer, and me, with the help of dear Dawn, who always came to the rescue when we were most in need. I'm not sure I'm eloquent enough to write about that moving experience. Bad? It was horrific, horrendous, awful, unspeakable —you name it. But the experience was life altering. Dana was, in a word, a disaster. If only we could have gotten rid of her for a few days.

Dawn, Boomer, and I made it, and we were in the new house. It marked a clean and total break from the past and in some ways clarified my role as a caregiver. I was now totally in charge of everything. Up until now our decision tree had many branches. We were feeling our way along, not knowing what to expect next. Decisions very often were made for medical reasons, for emotional reasons, for practical reasons, for whatever reason might have presented itself at the time. So much was going on in my mind that I hadn't taken the opportunity to make a master plan or even think if there could be a master plan when facing an uncharted landscape. As Lewis Carroll said: *If you don't know where you're going, any road will get you there.* Having bought the new house gave me a direction. The road would continue to be bumpy, but this experience was teaching me that when you're riding through hell, it's best to keep riding.

Dana was so mystified, confused, sullen, detached, out of sorts, and whatever else, she crawled into her mind and never really came back out. Her condition wasn't any worse than the days before the move; she was just so unfamiliar with her environment that she mentally removed herself from it. She could no longer cook anything nor did I want her to try because she might burn the house down. *She might burn the house down.* I could never leave her alone in the kitchen. I still tried to help her cook or bake occasionally, foolishly thinking it might turn into a good experience for her. Clearly, the move to a new house didn't improve her ability to follow a recipe or measure ingredients. I tried to help so she could do something rather than just sit and stare into space. Invariably the project would deteriorate into a frustrated shouting episode followed by an emotional, tearful period where somewhere deep inside she knew what was happening to her. It was so sad. My heart was breaking, and there was nothing I or anyone else could do.

She always liked doing the laundry, so I encouraged her to continue doing so. Laundry became one of the last activities she could attempt on her own, but the new washer and dryer were a major issue. She insisted on doing the laundry but required constant help to set the appliances. Sometimes clothes were washed without soap. Sometimes delicates were washed on the towel cycle. Hot water and hot drying often resulted in some of our clothes changing size. Either that or I was gaining weight. She got into the habit of turning the water to the washing machine on and off at the source. When the washer wouldn't work when she turned it on, there was an ensuing rage until I got the water turned back on.

From time to time I found my underwear in the pantry, socks in her underwear drawer, folded shirts in the linen closet—God only knows. It was partly humorous but also incredibly sad. She did her best, and there was no way I was going to complain or bring it to her attention. Searching for my underwear was a small price to pay for something that might make Dana happy. And ultimately most of our clothes were located.

Because of her limitations, doing the laundry filled considerable time and gave me a break knowing there was little trouble she could get into doing the laundry. She made a meal of getting the laundry done, but she looked forward to doing it almost every day—or at least it was something she thought about doing—and seemed to enjoy doing it. Far be it for me to criticize or discourage.

The bigger house gave me some room to breathe but presented more challenges for Dana to navigate. The house was two stories, and while everything we needed and virtually all our living was on the ground floor, the upstairs was a continuing mystery to Dana. Her infrequent ventures upstairs caused confusion and an occasional panic attack that required me to go upstairs to get her and spend some amount of time calming her down. That's another example of why she needed my constant supervision.

The new house had a beautiful park in front of it, an expanse of lawns surrounded a long and lovely shallow fountain. Multiple climbing roses in many gorgeous colors ornamented a formal, shaded pavilion with tables, chairs, and swings. And the distant view from the pavilion was the spectacular desert beauty of the Mc-Dowell Mountains, dotted with saguaro cactus. We could walk out our front door and enjoy this magnificent setting. I hoped it would be calming, serene, and reassuring for Dana. It was also a great place to take Boomer for a walk. I often tried to go into the park with Dana and Boomer just for a little walk or to sit on the swings. She seemed to enjoy it briefly but invariably got fidgety and wanted to go back inside. As her mind was closing in, I think she felt more comfortable in environments with boundaries.

Occasionally, she would take Boomer out for a walk "without" me. I couldn't let her be outside either alone or with the dog unattended. I always kept an eye on her, ensuring that she wouldn't wander away and not be able to find her way back—or, God forbid, lose Boomer. So while I thought our new home gave me more space, and indeed it did, it turned out that space wasn't the solution as I was still tethered to Dana 24/7. The Alzheimer's patient demands constant vigilance from the caregiver. You can't take your eye off them.

When I say YOU CAN'T TAKE YOUR EYE OFF THEM, *you probably equate that with the wisdom of parenting a toddler, because that was probably the last time you were engaged in this type of constant supervision and surveillance. This is similar, except that the toddler with Alzheimer's has access to electrical and gas appliances, alarm system codes, electronic equipment, and is fully capable of opening the front door or even grabbing the car keys. It's toddler mayhem in an adult body. And were they to escape and try to run goodness-knows-where, people will not be alarmed in the same way they would be seeing a toddler running on the loose in public. Or driving a car for that matter.*

The daily routine of getting up in the morning and getting ready for the day was becoming more complicated and time-consuming. In addition to the often hostile, confrontational exchanges over showering and brushing her teeth—often because she insisted she was already clean and minty fresh—getting dressed was the next battle of the day. Sometimes she didn't want to get out of her pajamas but most often was willing to get dressed although if left alone she'd wear the same unlaundered outfit every day.

Upon reflection, I should have let her. It would have solved two problems: I wouldn't have to fight her about what she wore, and I wouldn't have to search for her underwear! Contemporaneously, however, I wasn't that creative, so I battled with her over wearing the same thing she wore the day before, sometimes winning and sometimes losing. Winning is an unusual term to use because throughout all of these numerous upheavals and the daily struggles in Dana's disease, there are no wins. There are only losses. Nonetheless, if we got past wearing yesterday's clothes, I then confronted a new battle over what clothes she was going to wear today. I tried to give her the freedom to choose for two reasons: First, I hoped it would make her feel good. The less important second reason was that I could avoid yet another turbulent and brutal fight. The lady that was once a fashion plate wherever she went would now just as soon wear stripes with paisleys. I know it wasn't that she didn't care; it's because she didn't know.

Pick your battles. People with Alzheimer's lose all understanding of clothing in the fashion sense. They tend to be more sensitive to textures, preferring soft fabrics, and temperatures, with what seems to be an impossibly small comfort zone between too hot and too cold. Use mix-and-match items with layers such as cardigans or jackets that can be added or subtracted as needed. And try to stay practical. So what if they look odd? Much better to be comfortably dressed without emotional trauma. Keep it simple, keep it few, be flexible, and stay calm. Whatever is acceptable for comfort one minute will be uncomfortable five minutes later. As for the amount of clothing to choose from, with someone suffering from Alzheimer's, less is more— five mix and match outfits is plenty.

Next on the daily agenda came breakfast. By now I had learned not to ask what Dana wanted for breakfast. Her ability to make independent choices was so severely hampered that no good outcome came from free choice. I gave her what I hoped was a couple of acceptable options. I had learned that she could not handle more than two. If the first options didn't result in a hit, I'd give her a couple more until she settled on one.

Included in the decision process was whether I would fix something for her at home or take her and Boomer to the market and pick something up. As I explained earlier, the number of times we went to a restaurant for breakfast was few and far between. Having settled on what she wanted for breakfast, I proceeded to either fix it or fetch it.

When presented to her, she as often as not didn't want it, either having not remembered what we were going to have or having changed what was left of her mind but unable to communicate that change. After reiterating this process a couple of times, I'd finally get a cup of coffee and something to eat in her to start the day. Lunch and dinner were replays of breakfast. Suffice it to say, each meal was an exercise in exhaustion, with the simple enjoyment of a meal the least likely result. That repeated every day.

Despite how bad Dana was at restaurants, occasionally the mealtime wars literally drove me out of the house and to a restaurant to escape the kitchen battleground although the restaurant experience continued to worsen as well. Choosing a restaurant was the easy part; I chose. Dana didn't remember her favorite restaurants even though the names might have sounded familiar, nor did she recall any of her favorite dishes at those restaurants.

The dining experience began pleasantly enough with the obligatory cosmopolitan. It usually went downhill from there—ordering, sending back, re-ordering, exchanging my dinner for hers, explaining what she was eating, and listening to her complain about something she had eaten and enjoyed for years but did not recognize anymore. The food was either too hot or too cold, too hard or too soft, too big or too small. Dana had always had a good appetite, but she no longer ate very much when we went out to dinner. She couldn't seem to handle the hustle and bustle of the wait staff or the confusion over choices or just the different environment.

More than once—invariably, in the middle of dinner—she announced for all to hear that she had to go pee. Unable to find the restroom on her own, I would have to escort her there after explaining to the wait staff that we were just going to the restroom and would be back to finish our dinners. I didn't know then, and I never will know, what on earth she did in the restroom while I was waiting for her to come out. On the positive side I'll always be thankful that even though the wait was long, I never had to go in and either help or rescue her.

After dinner, whether carry-in or at a restaurant, the hours before bedtime passed slowly. Dana acquired sundowner's syndrome relatively early on. As the sun was setting, her personality became more sullen and her demeanor more combative. I could tell that she was tiring and bedtime was coming—but not soon enough. She'd sit at the kitchen island and be generally negative to any conversation or suggestion. Every evening I looked forward to the time when she agreed with the suggestion to go to bed.

Going to bed presented another set of challenges. Getting undressed, while a hassle, was not nearly as challenging as getting dressed, and choosing what nightclothes to wear was a snap compared with trying to put together an outfit in the morning. It didn't matter if she wore the same pajamas every night if that's what she wanted to do. After all, she drove me crazy washing clothes every day, so she could have clean pajamas every night with no hassle. Washing up, taking medications, brushing her teeth—I had dispensed with using mouthwash out of fear she would just swallow it—came with the usual confrontations. However, once I finally got her to bed, most of the time she fell asleep fairly quickly. Thank God. That was MY time. After a seemingly endless day, I finally had a chance to sit down and take a deep breath, trying not to reflect on the day or think about tomorrow. I just wanted to clear my mind, and I did everything I could to do so. I usually poured a glass of wine, maybe watched a little TV, read a little, visited with Boomer, and always ended the night taking Boomer for a midnight walk.

I didn't want to think about the days because they had all become the same. It was Groundhog Day. *Déjà vu* all over again. The major activities of every day were the same: The battle of getting up and getting ready for the day, the breakfast eruption, the lunch confrontation, the dinner campaign, and the nighttime war. There was never any peace and damn few ceasefires.

In between, the majority of Dana's time was spent sitting at the kitchen island staring off into space while I tried to engage her in anything I could think of, usually to no avail. With the possible exception of ALS (Lou Gehrig's disease), in my opinion, Alzheimer's is the worst hand a person and their caregivers can be dealt. Alzheimer's is turbulent, brutal, and unrelenting. It is death by a thousand cuts. There is nothing to look forward to. Again, the only thing that can be said with absolute certainty about Alzheimer's is that no matter how bad today might have been, tomorrow will be worse.

Sometimes I could get Dana's attention and occasionally calm her down by turning on some of her favorite music. Dana loved music and had a magnificent voice. Her good times during those weeks, months and years found her singing. While she was forgetting everything else, lyrics to songs seemed to be retained, not all the words but enough that she didn't notice. There were many occasions when I was at the end of my rope and thought I couldn't do this any longer. Then I'd hear Dana singing. That always improved the mood and put a little gas back in my tank. I guess I can say that some of the time Dana was sitting at the kitchen island was filled with her singing. It was far too little but every positive moment was precious and gave me something to hang my hat on.

You're going to be surprised, but music really is magic. People with Alzheimer's are often able to sing songs, apparently recalling the words with ease even when they cannot recall any other detail of their lives. Clinical studies in academic, peer-reviewed journals have reported that singing seems to unlock parts of the brain that are otherwise inaccessible, and listening to music can have a powerful, calming effect. We also know from the academic literature that hearing is the last of the senses to leave us as we approach the end of life. That's why staff in critical care areas of hospitals is careful about what they say in the presence of their sickest patients. Be mindful and deeply respectful of the power of music. It may be able to help when nothing else can reach the one you love.

As the months wore on, I even had to curtail Dana's evening cocktail or glass of wine after I noticed that if we opened a bottle of wine and each had a glass, the next day the bottle was empty. And the level of the vodka bottle I kept in the freezer kept getting lower and lower. Whenever I asked Dana about it, she flew into a rage, taking it that I was accusing her of drinking too much and being an alcoholic.

I could explain the wine in my mind. She might not have remembered having her glass of wine and had helped herself to another when I was out of sight. The vodka was another issue because she had never mixed her own cosmopolitan. The answer came during one of Dawn's visits to help me get through a couple of days. Dawn saw Dana open the freezer, take a big swig from the bottle of vodka, and then put the bottle back. I knew better than to confront Dana, but I'll never know why she was doing that. Maybe it just made her feel better. It couldn't have been that it would help her forget. She couldn't remember anything anyway.

Dana's drinking habits forced a change in mine. I curtailed the cosmos and white wine considerably. I would have my glass of wine after Dana went to bed. I know she wasn't dependent on alcohol because when I cut it down, got rid of the vodka in the freezer, and just didn't open another bottle of wine, there was no discussion. She didn't ask about it and didn't seem to either need it or miss it. Going forward, I was able to manipulate the drinking so she could enjoy a glass of wine with dinner and leave it at that. It took careful planning and execution, a little sleight of hand, and a little lying, but we got the drinking under control.

Chapter 8:
Help/Hope Is on the Way

Two years post diagnosis...

For several years I have been on the board of directors of one of the Federal Home Loan Banks. The position requires me to travel to various locations around the country for board meetings. Without help, I had no alternative but to take Dana with me. As described earlier, travel with Dana was an absolute nightmare, but it had to be done.

I was very lucky that the spouses of the other directors were sympathetic to my situation and were willing to keep an eye on Dana while I was tied up in meetings. Even then, the numerous and usual daily battles didn't change. If anything, they were a little worse because the confusion of a new environment complicated things. Dana escaped on a couple of occasions but was found each time without major incident—except for my frazzled nerves.

I realized that traveling with Dana to bank meetings was not going to work much longer. I had to find a way to leave her at home or take a companion for her with us. The latter seemed the best solution; there was no way I could leave her alone with someone else. There were too many unknown variables, and it was just too much responsibility to put on someone's shoulders who wouldn't know how to fight the battles and deflect, disarm, defer, and diffuse her increasing eccentricities. Besides, Dana wouldn't stand for me not being there 24/7. While she continued to battle with me and abuse me at every junction, she was insistent that she always be with me, that I always be there.

The idea of traveling with someone to help was about to be put to the test. Dana and I had gone to Hawaii a number of times. She enjoyed every trip there. We had always had a great and relaxing time. Since travel was becoming so difficult, I thought one last trip to Hawaii—with help and support—might be a good idea. Plus, I thought it would be beneficial to Dana's state of mind, and for old-time's sake, for her to enjoy what would probably be her last trip of this nature. I wanted so badly to do something with her and for her that might bring some joy and comfort.

We made a plan for Dawn and my son-in-law Mark, my son Greg, and my daughter-in-law Lael to accompany Dana and me to Maui for ten days. It would be a great time. We would relax, take Dana for walks on the beach, go out to dinner, and enjoy each other in the beauty of paradise. The kids could surf and hike and do things they liked as well. But we would all be together—a time for bonding. And I would have them around to help with Dana if needed. I arranged for a condo on the beach and got the airline tickets. All Dawn and Mark, Greg and Lael had to do was get from Denver to Scottsdale.

The day came, and we were off to Maui. The airport wasn't too bad at all. Everyone pitched in to get through the post-911 security struggles. Dana was a little agitated and confused, but we made it through and onto the airplane. My kids helped a lot through the airport. The plane ride was somewhat better than I anticipated, thanks in part to some sedatives I got Dana to take.

We landed in Maui, picked up our two rental cars, found our way to the condo, checked in, and got our luggage unloaded and into the condo. Dana was bewildered. She had no idea where we were or why we were there. She became agitated, paranoid, and anxious. As I should have expected, one of her panic attacks ensued. As it subsided, she was even more confused and became hysterical. I had some calming medication prescribed for her periods of anxiety. I got it down her and tried to wait out the episode. The next several hours were among the worst of my life. Her condition didn't improve and was not going to improve. I can only imagine her terror.

Clearly, I had made a mistake. Dana and I were on a plane back to Phoenix the next morning. I insisted that the kids stay and enjoy the trip as much as they could. Once home, I was able to get Dana settled and to bed. When she awoke, she had no recollection of the events of the prior forty-eight hours, and I saw no reason to resurrect them.

Lesson learned.

Dana's doctors later told me that jet lag is very real and extremely pronounced in Alzheimer's patients. Time zone changes and new environments at the same time are confusing and bewildering. They advised me to limit any future air travel for Dana to no more than one or two time zones away. I decided that there would be no future air travel of this nature, except for the possible exception of bank board meetings, which would be difficult but would cross only one or two time zones. The Maui experience was enough to last a lifetime.

This is going to sound cruel, but it's not meant to be cruel. This is wisdom borne of pain, as the song lyrics say. As much as you may want to take that last, big trip you had always talked and dreamed about, or a trip for old time's sake, that ship has already sailed. People with Alzheimer's are using every ounce of their energy and every shred of their effort to deal with here and now, this place and this minute. Travel on a grand scale will cause them unimaginable distress. It causes the same measure of distress to the caregiver, and you may never get over it. The sufferer forgets but you may not. It's true and inescapable.

So, the picture was now becoming much clearer. The new, bigger house was not the solution. The amount of space wasn't the problem, only a minor inconvenience when compared to the larger problem. What my personal Mayo physician, Dr. Kenworthy, had been telling me for some time finally started to sink in. She had encouraged me, browbeat me, and prescribed for me to get some help. She preached that I couldn't care for Dana alone. She took me by the figurative throat, told me that Dana's ship was sinking, and she would not allow me to go down with it.

At first I agreed help was probably the answer. I later learned help was definitely the answer—and not just occasional help. I thought I wouldn't need a lot of help, just occasional help. Enough help to give me a break now and then. I still justified that the new, larger house was going to make having help easier. I had mostly wanted the space so I could get away inside the house as well as out. But if the time came when I needed live-in help, there would be room available.

With the ever-present guidance and assistance from my friends at the Mayo Clinic, particularly, Dr. Anne Kenworthy, my patron saint sent from heaven, along with research on the Internet, I started contacting home healthcare agencies. Dr. Kenworthy recommended a couple of individuals as well who provided that sort of care and support, but they were already overworked and had waiting lists. I discovered later that good caregivers are rare and in incredible demand.

Through research and recommendations, I narrowed my search to three possibilities. Interviewing came next, and it was a handful having candidates come to the house to interview because Dana wanted to know what was going on. I tried my best to explain that we needed some help with housekeeping, cooking, laundry she blew a gasket at this suggestion, telling everyone in no uncertain terms that laundry was off limits—running errands, etc.

I explained that help would make our life more leisurely for us, but Dana fought it all the way. She was adamant we needed NO help, and she didn't want anyone coming to our home snooping around (paranoia) and doing things that were none of their business. Point made. Dana was severely challenged, but she knew something was going on that she didn't like. It wasn't passing her smell test. Interviewing and hiring help to come into the house was a MAJOR battle.

By the way, make sure that you have homeowners' liability insurance that will cover incidents that could occur with contracted workers coming into your home. This must include both agency help and any people you may hire as independent contractors. If you ever happen to hire someone as an employee, make sure you acquire workers' compensation coverage.

I chose the company that made the best presentation and looked like the best fit. Now, the job was to select the actual caregiver(s). I interviewed several caregivers—getting the presence, look, and demeanor right is critical or using a caregiver will never work with the demented mind—before settling on a young girl named Desiree who was pleasant and non-threatening to Dana.

For the first several visits, Dana wanted nothing to do with Desiree and wanted her to leave. The visits were confrontational and awkward; however, after a few weeks Dana came to accept her. Desiree would come three or four times a week for three or four hours each time to give me a break. Her assigned duties were to visit with Dana, help with her makeup, look at magazines, play music—to just try and occupy her.

Let's be clear: She wasn't hired for Dana; she was hired for *me!* Unfortunately, Desiree had another job at a fast food restaurant and started coming to work late or not at all because of scheduling conflicts. Of greater concern was that she wasn't very good at occupying Dana. At first I ignored her shortcomings, tried to work *us* into *her* schedule, and hoped it would work out. I really wanted the help and didn't particularly want to go through the pain and agony of another search to find someone else. It was hard enough getting Dana to accept Desiree, and the battle to introduce a new player should be avoided if possible. That was my thinking at the time, anyway, flawed as it was.

You can only pick a scab so many times until you tire of the bleeding. I was paying the agency $50/hour for Desiree, a burger flipper. The home health care agency Desiree worked for paid her $10/hour. It doesn't take a rocket scientist to realize that a $10/hour worker is not up to the task of taking care of an Alzheimer's victim. Hell, someone who was worth $50/hour would be stretched to get their arms around the task.

I hired the same agency to send more qualified caregivers through an enhanced package that cost significantly more and still delivered significantly less. In a nutshell, I agreed to look at their nursing option. The result was them sending a licensed practical nurse (LPN) and charging for a registered nurse. Imagine what you get in an LPN working for less than the going rate being charged out at double the going rate. It didn't take much of this nonsense for me to cut my losses. That plan was clearly not the answer either.

In-home, part-time assistance was painful and agonizing to get started and clumsy to live with. It produced little or no results and had no long-term benefits for either Dana or me. I had to work harder and was more engaged than I was without the help. I needed help, but the business model that sells you a part-time burger flipper and charges professional rates for Alzheimer's care was not going to work for us. Quite frankly, it's hard to believe that it would work at all. It's also amazing that it can be sold as a solution or that people buy it. You want and need help so badly that you grasp at straws. You accept almost anything, thinking that something is better than nothing. Worse yet, I didn't want to go through the painful experience of trying to find another solution, yet this something was not better than nothing! Companies flourish taking advantage of a large demand fighting for a limited supply of qualified caregivers.

I was back to square one. I still needed help, and now I *wanted* help. I was beginning to feel desperate. Even though Desiree never relieved me from the major morning, noon, and nighttime issues of the day, after having just a few hours a week to do something other than watch Dana I really realized that I needed some relief. But I needed better relief as well.

There's a lot going on here, right? Lots of moving parts and no easy answers. Some of you are probably struggling to identify with someone who is devastated by the failure of part-time hired help, especially if that's never going to be an option for you financially or otherwise. I get it. But here's the point: you will eventually recognize you're in over your head, you're utterly exhausted, and you don't know how you'll make it through today, let alone tomorrow. You need help, but more than that you need to understand that you deserve help.

Although your exhausted self may just want to run and hide, you need to do the exact opposite; you need to reach out and connect with your community. Find the resources in respite care that can help you, especially in your faith community, in your city government social services network, the local chapter of the Alzheimer's Association, and even your medical care network of hospitals and physicians. The reason is simple: these folks handle situations like yours every day, and they want to help. This is the first time you have experienced this—and hopefully the only time—but there are people in your community who are trained and willing to help.

Back to our story and part-time help. You will learn—either here by reading this or the hard way through experience—that hiring any

*kind of help requires a very disciplined, clear-eyed, hard-nosed, busi-
ness-like approach. You're desperate and emotionally and physically
exhausted. You often arrive at this moment after a sudden deterio-
ration in your loved one's condition, and your need is immediate and
urgent. Don't let your distressed mindset make poor decisions. Force
yourself to think slowly and carefully while moving as quickly as is
reasonable, and the minute something feels off, stop. You're going to
learn to depend on your inner voice and your instincts, so start trust-
ing them now.*

After a few weeks without part-time help, Dr. Kenworthy called
to tell me she knew someone who might be a fit for Dana. It wasn't
a friend of hers but a distant acquaintance she knew from her children's school. If I was interested, she would mention it to her acquaintance, Sherri. I jumped at the prospect. I knew I didn't like
the home healthcare agency model of sending a cheap laborer and
charging a professional rate; however, I was still most interested in
a personal, in-home model of care.

Telephone calls were made, visits were conducted over the
phone, and an interview meeting was scheduled at a coffee shop.
Sherri called me the day of the interview to tell me her husband
was coming with her because he wanted to meet me. I always
thought I was a smart guy. I clearly didn't see this one coming.

*See? This is how your judgment gets clouded when you fight the
constant battles of caregiving without relief, want any relief you can
get, and don't want to go through the search process again. At the
outset something was not right. But the prospect of help and relief
stepped in front of those warnings from instincts. What could possibly go wrong?*

I met Sherri and her husband Brian, a former police officer who
had retired because of a disability although for all the time I came
to know him I didn't detect any discernible disability. The interview
was pleasant enough. I got to know Sherri, and Brian got to know

me. Sherri was a pleasant, attractive lady. She was engaging, nicely dressed, and relatively articulate. By this I mean she could string several sentences together and form them into a coherent expression of thought. I liked Sherri—or really wanted to like her—and felt that Dana could come to like her as well.

I explained what I was looking for. I wanted someone to help me with Dana forty hours a week. My experience with part-time help had convinced me more time was needed. I wanted her to have flexibility in hours and days. Ideally, I wanted morning hours some days to help get Dana ready for the day, some mid-day hours to help with lunch or to take Dana out to lunch from time to time, and some evening hours to cover dinner and occasionally bedtime. I wanted her to schedule nail and hair appointments when needed for Dana and to take her to the nail and hair salon—all the things I had been doing but about as well as a fish without a bicycle.

Shopping was another request. I thought she could relieve me from shopping for things like bras. Hygiene, eating, medication, shopping, friend, companion, dog walking—you name it. I wanted and needed someone to connect with Dana, be committed to Dana, protect Dana, support her, help her, and be her guardian angel. And I was willing to pay for it. I already knew that trying to save money on caregiving was, how do you say, a losing proposition.

Sherri was attentive, made several salient points, asked good questions, was understanding, seemed compassionate, and felt she could do the job.

By the way, I had a neighbor watch Dana while I went to the interview; I didn't leave her home alone with Boomer. I could go nowhere and leave her alone. Clearly, I needed help.

I was excited, and Sherri seemed excited as well. She appeared to be the perfect fit; her personality was outgoing and friendly, yet warm. Her appearance was one Dana could identify with. If it worked out, I would introduce her slowly, feeling that her personality would do the rest to disarm Dana's apprehensions about having someone around she thought she didn't need and certainly did not want.

I told Sherri I wanted to hire her, and she said she would like to have the job. She had been working part-time in a high school cafeteria and could use something better. Even with my prior experience with fry cooks, I thought Sherri was the solution. She was mature, calm, professional, and her job in the cafeteria was to get tuition paid for her children who attended the expensive private school where Sherri worked—better than flipping burgers. I really didn't want to make another mistake. I needed and wanted help, and the agony and effort of going through his exercise again was to be avoided if at all possible. Better yet, she could start immediately. Hopefully, she could be one of those rare good caregivers, and I could be lucky enough to land her without being put on a waiting list.

The interview turned into a hiring meeting where I reiterated what I wanted in spades. Sherri was confident she could do the job. Next was to settle on compensation. As we discussed the financial arrangements, her husband Brian became considerably more active in the discussion. This intrusion into what until then was a normal and reasonable employment interview was unwelcome and offensive. Normally I would have suggested to Brian that he might want to excuse himself while Sherri and I discussed our potential business arrangement, but those weren't normal times for me. I liked Sherri and I knew how hard it was to look for, interview, and hire someone to help me with Dana. I assessed that Brian might have a short fuse and would blow the entire deal if I were to upset him, so I stifled my better judgment and the discussion continued.

Signal #2 noticed but ignored! Clouded judgment is a consequence of the toll taken by 24/7/365 caregiving. It takes strength, discipline, and resolve to consider your instincts when all else is crumbling around you.

I had paid $50/hour to an agency for unacceptable part-time help. A rate of $50/hour for forty hours a week is $100,000 a year. I didn't think Sherri was worth that, even though I thought the job was almost priceless for the right person. We finally settled for $25/hour plus a bonus arrangement to be determined as we were able to establish benchmarks and success points that could be measured.

That was probably more than either of them had ever earned. Be cautious about making foolish decisions as much as wrong decisions.

As the meeting was about to conclude, Brian interjected that he thought Sherri should be paid a sum of money up front as a show of good will that I was sincere and real and to help her until her first payday. My knee-jerk reaction was to tell him he couldn't possibly be serious but at this point I knew that he was. I had already gone further than my instincts would normally have allowed, but by swallowing my pride to finish the hire and hopefully find someone to help me, I let him take advantage of the momentary weakness and agreed to pay her $800 as an advance on her first paycheck. Whew!! The good news is that the $800 advance was repaid in Sherri's first paycheck.

Sherri was hired and help—and hope—was on the way. Introducing Sherri to Dana went slowly and relatively smoothly. I was encouraged. After a few visits Dana liked her, and Sherri seemed to like Dana. Sherri took off running. She could get Dana to do things that were great struggles for me. Dana seemed to want to please Sherri, and her mood visibly improved around Sherri. That was a great relief to me. I could leave the house or do things in and around the house without the pressure of constant vigilance. I was able to breathe deeply for the first time in a long time. Dana actually looked forward to Sherri's visits.

The mornings with Sherri were so much more pleasant than the mornings when I fought the battle alone. Dana looked so much better when the morning routine was handled with Sherri. Her makeup was nice, her hair was combed much better, and her clothes were more put together. Hell, Dana even let Sherri help with doing the laundry!

Sherri took Dana to get her hair and nails done, and they would stop to get mint-chocolate chip ice cream on the way. The mood was bright and cheery when they came home. The outings were a success! Sherri and Dana went to lunch occasionally and came back in great moods. Occasionally Sherri took a nap with Dana. Prior to nodding off, Sherri would play some music on Dana's iPad, play a little game with her, or just visit about nothing. I often found them singing together. It was like a sleepover with a friend. They talked about Dana's mother and dad, her old real estate business, and her children and granddaughters. I'm sure Dana mostly faked her side of the conversations. Except for remembering her mother, Nurse Bonnie, she remembered little else at this point. When they got up or when I returned home if I had been gone, the mood was improved over what I had been experiencing. I was becoming happier and happier with Sherri and her integration into Dana's care.

Having some alone evening time was particularly enjoyable for me. I could go to a movie or have dinner and a glass of wine without confrontation and constant battles. When I returned home after the few evenings I had out, I often found Dana in bed with Sherri sleeping next to her like sisters. What a joy and relief; she was in bed sleeping, and I didn't have to fight to get it done. Because of Sherri's family obligations, free evenings for me were still relatively rare. Brian didn't want Sherri out after dark, and she still had two school-aged daughters—one in high school and one in junior high. Her other two children were a son living at home trying to become a fireman and a daughter also living at home trying to find work.

Sherri's children, particularly the ones in school, were active, and Sherri was involved in their lives as she should have been. We were pretty successful in balancing her home life with Dana's care in scheduling her work hours. Conflicts arose but were solved with some cooperation. After all, I didn't care when I got relief; I just needed relief. If it was Wednesday rather than Monday, that was no big deal. The objective remained to involve her in Dana's care forty hours a week and to have that care sprinkled throughout the day to cover not only the daily pressure points but to also take Dana out of the house for all the chores and activities that could be better done with another woman rather than with me.

While still challenging and difficult, life was better than it had been in months—or years for that matter. Dana's future was still bleak, but it felt like I was at least beginning to tread water or stop taking it on so much. Relief had come. Sherri even accompanied us to bank board meetings in Kansas City, Coeur d'Alene, Idaho, and Sea Island, Georgia. Her help was great navigating airports, taxis, and hotels. I could get my work done without the stress of worrying about Dana or inconveniencing the other directors' spouses. Sherri was happy. She earned a great deal of money traveling to lovely destinations with all her expenses paid, and most importantly Dana was safe and secure. Life would never be the same again, but I had a glimmer that it might be incrementally more tolerable going forward.

Looking back now, we went along for a considerable time with me ignoring some nagging little things and abrasive eccentricities I noticed. I went to lunch with Dana and Sherri one day. Sherri drove. When we arrived at the restaurant, Sherri didn't pull directly into the parking spot but drove past and backed in—clumsily, I might add. When prodded, she told me that Brian would not allow her or their kids to park front in. They were instructed to always back in so that they could make a quick getaway if necessary. I laughed, but she wasn't joking. She said that he would go into a furious rage if he ever found out they had disobeyed that rule. In fact, she said that if he knew where they were, he was prone to check on them to make sure they did as instructed.

Over the course of getting to know Sherri, I learned that she and Brian, as well as all their children, had concealed weapon permits, and they always had their heat with them. Think that made me sleep better at night?? I was reassured somewhat that they were regulars at the shooting range.

Because there's nothing strange or abnormal about weaponized home help, RIGHT?

I also learned that all of their savings, however much that might have been, was in gold coins and bars kept in a huge safe in their home. Brian didn't trust banks, stocks, bonds, or it appeared, anything or anyone. Once, when I picked Sherri up because one of her children was using her car, Brian—who was always lurking—invited me in to show me the safe. Sure enough, it was a big-un.

So, we're placing implicit trust in a lurking family with trust issues bigger than all outdoors. Run, Forrest, run!

These idiosyncrasies caused me concern, but I was willing to ignore them, hoping they wouldn't offend my sensibilities to where I'd have to make another change in caregivers. I sincerely wanted Sherri to work out. It was the only peace I had experienced for I couldn't remember how long. She simply had to succeed.

With all of this going on, you're looking away from things that are trying to get your attention. Don't do this.

Since Sherri was taking Dana to lunch occasionally, I was happy to buy her lunch as well. I told her just to use the credit card I had given her to cover things for Dana. It was the right thing to do.

As the months went by, Sherri and Dana were going to lunch much more often. And there was a change in her visit pattern. More and more often she came by in the morning to pick Dana up, saying she was taking Dana to see her daughter perform or to a dancing recital, or she had to pick up her kids from school and wanted Dana to go along or was taking Dana to her house that day. In the beginning it seemed innocent enough. It even seemed healthy for Dana to be out and about to some extent.

But as I became increasingly attuned to the pattern change, it became clear that Sherri was conducting her personal business, living her family life, doing what she needed or wanted to do—supporting her children, running Brian's errands—and dragging Dana along. Dana was no longer the priority; she was a passenger along for the ride through Sherri's life. All the while I was paying Sherri to live her life with only the annoyance of having to pick up someone to go along. Her attention to Dana steadily decreased.

Lunches, however, continued to increase. And the lunch bills got bigger and bigger. It seems that Sherri would order a huge lunch for Dana—much more than she could possibly eat—and a large lunch for herself. Leftovers were taken home to feed Brian and the kids. Swell! Now Dana's care was compromised by Sherri's family business and activities, I was feeding the whole family, and I was paying her for ever-increasing hours since she was taking Dana everywhere with her. Pretty good gig if you can be provided food and be paid for just living your life as you ordinarily would.

The clarifying moment came when I took Sherri out to dinner with Dana and me one evening after she brought Dana home after a hard day at the office. At dinner I ordered both Dana and me a salad. Sherri ordered prime rib—the large cut—with a couple of sides. She barely touched her dinner and at the end of the meal asked for take-home boxes. I can still see Brian eating prime rib that evening. I'm convinced he had pressured her into the lunch gig assuming I was too dumb to notice. He was a classical *smartest guy in the room.*

I had been very nice and incredibly generous to Sherri. During her tenure I listed our condo to sell and gave her much of the furniture I didn't move into our new house, including the washer and dryer. At one point she begged me for a loan. Against my better judgment, I lent her $5,000, which to her credit she paid back out of future paychecks. I did everything I could to make our arrangement work. My relief was so great I know now that I would have done almost anything to make the arrangement work. Even with the many lunches and the dinner episode along with the strange pattern of behavior, I justified that the cost was worth it. I also justified that while Dana was a lower priority with Sherri than I should have expected her to be and that she should have been, I felt that she was safe, and I was able to have some peace. And I thought that Sherri really liked Dana.

The desperate need for relief from the exhaustion of constant caregiving was offset and measured against the knowledge that the quality of relief care violated all of my personal and business standards and instincts. Add to that the growing abhorrence at the thought of yet another search and hiring process, and you have some idea of the guilt/outrage paradox I was experiencing.

Sherri, most likely prodded by Brian, traded on my generosity and need versus the possibility that I was stupid. I've been called many things, but stupid has never been among them. I was aware of this innocent pretending, presumptuous, familiar sense of entitlement. I had experienced it before in other relationships. These kinds of relationships always begin on a high note with high hopes. They degrade over time and challenge the patience of the offended. My patience was being put to the test, but when weighed against the alternative, I was willing to take another deep breath and swallow. I really didn't want to go through the agony of introducing another player into Dana's care. Not only would it be hard on me, but it also would be traumatic and very disruptive to Dana. So we continued.

I was still troubled by Sherri's taking advantage, primarily because Dana's care was taking the back seat. When she was on the job, her primary focus should be on Dana, not on getting her daughters to their music lessons. While this percolated in my mind, one day I got a call from Dana's hairstylist, Stephanie. She was frazzled. Luckily, Dana's phone was in her purse, and my name was at the top of the favorites list. Stephanie told me that some young girl and her boyfriend had brought Dana to have her hair done but did not return to pick her up.

I was aware that Sherri was taking Dana to have her hair done that day, so I wasn't surprised that she was at the salon. I *was* surprised—surprised is probably not the right word; livid would be closer—that someone other than Sherri took her. Orders were that Dana would always be in Sherri's—and only Sherri's—care. That wasn't a responsibility that could be fulfilled by a subcontractor.

I immediately knew what was going on. Sherri had something better to do, so she had one of her daughters take Dana to the hairdresser. As it turned out, it was her sixteen-year-old-just-learning-how-to-drive with her boyfriend along daughter. They took her to the hair salon, dumped her off, and either forgot to come back for her or just didn't bother to. I told Stephanie to keep her eye on Dana, and I would be there in ten minutes. Fortunately, I was already in my car when I took the call and was only ten or fifteen minutes away from the salon.

On my way I called Sherri and fired her over the phone before she could even attempt to offer any excuse. What she did was inexcusable. I told her that the last check she got from me was her last. I was livid! After the firing, I still had most of the ten minutes to go and rescue Dana. I had no interest in anything Sherri might have tried to say.

I don't know what I might have done had this egregious episode not happened. I'll never know how many other times Sherri had substituted someone other than herself for Dana's care. I'm sure this wasn't the first. Her presumptuous behavior had become increasingly evident, and I had done nothing about it out of fear of losing the help. Having been caught this time in such an unforgivable position gave me the opportunity and the courage to stop the nonsense and do what had to be done. Sherri was history, and this chapter in Dana's care was firmly closed. As bad as it was, and as badly as it ended, Sherri's tenure taught me the value of help in Dana's care. It also confirmed to me that this enhanced model of in-home personal care was not the solution either.

This is extremely serious, but it could have been worse. In fact, it could have been life-threatening in a different set of circumstances. This is the inevitable outcome of letting a bad hiring decision become toxic and not correcting that decision, despite numerous warning signs. Never lose sight of the duty to protect your loved one. They are utterly defenseless in the face of Alzheimer's, and therefore everyone involved in their care must be fully accountable and responsive to their needs EVERY SINGLE MINUTE. The only dim light in this nightmare scenario is that Dana was not physically harmed or hopefully even aware of the problem, but her lack of awareness simply magnifies the neglect. If you're not convinced that the people caring for your Alzheimer's sufferer don't share your level of care and concern, get rid of them NOW! This awful situation is a powerful reminder that your instincts will always have the last word.

I was back in the saddle again. It was time to suck it up, go back to 24/7/365, create a new plan, and keep on riding. How bad could it get? The good news was that I was having no luck selling our condo in Scottsdale. This was good only on a relative scale. I needed to get the condo sold and was having no luck in doing so. It was draining time and energy I didn't have. It was really bad news, but not as bad as starting 24/7/365 caregiving without help and trying to figure out what I was going to do next.

As I thought about where to turn next for direction and help, I reflected on where we had been and what I had learned about the hired help we had. Part-time help provided by an agency charging premium rates for minimum wage workers didn't work. The same agency sending more qualified caregivers and charging more money didn't solve the problem. Full-time help worked early on until the relationship degraded because of entitlement and greed.

The lessons learned were that the home healthcare agency is to be avoided as a model that sends under-qualified, unsupervised employees and charges premium rates until you find out that you aren't getting what you are paying for. Their success relies on their obscene margins and high demand for their services. They can make enough money from enough people in the short-run to tide them over until the next sucker comes along. This model can only succeed in the long run because the supply of sick, aging people is almost limitless.

The almost limitless demand for home healthcare agencies is both a sign and a symptom of the problem. Their detached, unaccountable, irresponsible attitude can only exist in a market where there is a huge demand for their services and inadequate resources to meet that demand. WHY SHOULD THEY CARE if they fail you, disappoint you, or prove unreliable? If they destroy their relationship with you, they simply move to the next name on their waiting list, so don't expect remedy or remorse in this purely seller's market. This important concept cannot be overstated.

The availability of individual caregivers, the Sherri model, could work if there were enough good ones out there. The good ones are a treasure but are very rare, and their time is full. If they are available, you probably don't want them. If they're good, you can't get them. Success with this model was/is contingent on waiting a long time for availability or being damn lucky. Or both.

I was at the point where I couldn't wait and wasn't willing to try my luck again. So what to do? The experiences I'd had with caregivers over the previous couple of years and the miserable experience of finding and hiring changed my perspective about the possibility of having live-in help, which would have all the problems associated with the agency and individual caregiver models, plus more. I would still be a prisoner in my own home, would have no privacy, and no alone time at home. I would have to deal with a stranger coming and going—there was just no way.

Providing space for a live-in helper/caregiver had seemed like a good idea at the time, but the shine was definitely off that coin now. Buying the new home with this as one of the possibilities was the kind of decision made by an unknowing, bewildered, and inexperienced caregiver who is flopping around and grasping at any straws out there to help relieve the burden and manage this awful disease.

Additionally, research confirmed that *good* live-in help is the most expensive form of hired caregiving there is, and you still have periods—days off, holidays, vacation, evenings out, doctor appointments—when you'll be shoved into the breech as the primary caregiver. Hired in-home healthcare in any form did not appear to be a solution that fit my view of the world for these and many more reasons.

What to do?

Chapter 9:
Borrow Enough Money to Get Out of Debt

Four years post diagnosis...

Again taking care of Dana alone, over several weeks I thought and prayed and visited with her doctors and my doctors. The solution prescribed by the doctors and confirmed by Dana's deteriorating condition, my prior experiences, and our financial position—supplemented by long-term care insurance I had been smart enough to buy many years earlier—pointed to a nursing home as the solution. Preferably it would be one with both assisted living and memory care facilities and capabilities.

That was the lowest point in my decision making for Dana's care and was the most difficult decision I had ever faced in my life. It was the most profound decision that can be made by anyone for a loved one. It was a decision that would significantly alter Dana's life forever as well as mine. A decision she could not participate in.

Actually, Dana's life as everyone knew it and as she lived it had sadly ended long ago.

Just considering moving Dana out of her house and into a nursing home was antithetical to everything I had hoped to represent as a man. Love, duty, honor, trust, and commitment were how I tried to live my life. I had promised Dana to take care of her and to always be with her and by her side as long as I was able. Was I going back on that promise, or was I no longer able? I couldn't answer that question then, I can't answer it now, and I may never be able to answer it.

I began my research on nursing homes. I read a lot, surfed the net, and made several phone calls. I visited with my friends at the Mayo Clinic and got their input, advice, and some direction about nursing homes they had some experience with. Over Dana's vociferous objection and with the anticipation of several ugly confrontations when the time came, I arranged for a neighbor to watch Dana from time to time so I could visit nursing homes. From the very smallest to the very largest, old and new, there was one overriding impression—depressing.

The smallest facilities I visited were regular residential homes converted to a care facility with four to ten residents. I saw some that were very nice and some that were disgusting. They were all extremely depressing. Most the residents were wheelchair bound, sitting in front of a television unable to feed themselves and looking like they were just in a holding pattern for the mortuary. That was not for Dana. It was not appropriate for her condition. She was irascible and hostile, and she had lost considerable cognitive ability, but she was far from a holding pattern, and she was twenty-five years younger than anyone I saw.

I started to concentrate on larger facilities with seemingly big professional staffs, brighter accommodations, and more activities. They all started to look alike, and they all said the same things. Their marketing efforts were first-rate, and they led prospects to believe they were the answer to all your needs. Listening to them in the sales cycle would convince you that your search and worries were over. If they had been a bank, they would have convinced you that they could and would lend you enough money to get you completely out of debt.

Be on high alert from this point onwards for things that sound too good to be true. Most often they are.

Still, a decision had to be made, and I was frustrated, confused, and really down. I was as low as I could get and conflicted about moving Dana into a nursing home. I thought it couldn't get any worse. Wrong!

Returning home from a nursing home tour, I found Dana was not feeling well. She was experiencing anxiety and said she was going to vomit. I could see one of her panic attacks coming on, so I gave her one of the pills the doctors prescribed to help calm her down. This time, however, she did throw up, causing her really to go off the rails. I couldn't seem to calm her as I had in the past, plus she complained of a stomach ache. It started to look like a virus. I called the doctor's office for direction, and they told me to bring her in.

Going to the doctor was not what she had in mind, particularly in her present condition and state of mind. It was a battle, but I got her in the car and to the doctor. After considerable arguing the doctor got her to lie down on the exam table.

Dr. Kenworthy touched Dana's abdomen once, looked at me, and said, "We have a hot appendix; get her to the emergency room!"

I didn't take the time to tell her, "You can't be serious."

I helped get Dana dressed, got her to the car, and drove to the Mayo Clinic Hospital emergency room. We were met at the door. Dana was placed on a gurney and rolled into an exam room. She had no clue what was going on, but that didn't stop her from objecting to and struggling with everything that was happening or going to happen over the next few hours.

It was late afternoon when we got to the emergency room and about midnight when they rolled her into the operating room. I was exhausted. We had just gone through several of the most turbulent, agonizing hours of my life. You'd think I was numb to this roller coaster.

Surgery was successful and uneventful. The appendix had not burst, and Dana's prognosis from the surgery was positive; however, recovering from the anesthesia was a different matter. In my experience, Alzheimer's is a downward progression with a few cliffs that the victim falls off from time to time before resuming their slide. Undergoing a general anesthetic is one of those cliffs. It results in a severe setback the Alzheimer's patient never fully recovers from. The steady progression downward simply resumes from a much lower point than before. Bad as she had been, Dana was noticeably worse after her surgery.

Pain management is difficult in dementia patients. You don't know if you're treating current pain, the flawed memory of past pain, or anticipated pain. Dana described her pain post-surgery as "the worst pain I have ever had," and it lasted for weeks, coming and going randomly. It made her more irritated, more hostile, and harder to handle and care for than ever before. It was three or four months before the complaints of excruciating pain started to subside.

It seemed as if she could experience it on command, although she would have no reason to do so. She'd be sitting at the kitchen island and start complaining of the pain, telling me she could hardly stand it and that it was there all the time. Five minutes later I would ask how she was feeling, and she'd say that she was feeling fine. Pain was in her memory somewhere, sometime. It would come to the surface unexpectedly and at almost any time. The memory or lack thereof is a complete mystery and totally unmanageable and frustrating. As a caregiver you never know if your loved one's expressed pain is real or imagined from a distant memory.

I had learned to navigate the turbulence in Dana's care and come to understand and reluctantly accept that each succeeding day would be worse than the preceding, but the unexpected gut punch out of the dark in this case appendicitis—was always ... well, unexpected.

Alzheimer's care invariably involves the realization that you never get used to the body blows it delivers.

Another body blow when least needed and least deserved. Don't let the body blows get you down. Life continues, and so must you.

The appendicitis attack and ensuing experience were a turning point in my decision-making process regarding nursing homes. It clarified my thinking and strengthened my resolve that moving her to a nursing home was the right thing to do, notwithstanding my promise to take care of her at home for as long as I was able. If I took care of her much longer, I wouldn't be around to continue. As Dana progressed in her recovery, she was resistant to let me out of her sight to resume my search for a nursing home with the neighbor friend looking after her, but I doggedly resumed the search.

I finally found a place that stood out above the others and seemed a good candidate, Villa del Sol. I visited Villa several times to meet the staff and get a feeling for the culture, level of care, and general atmosphere. It seemed like a great fit. It was a beautiful place. Relatively new, it looked like a desert resort with an indoor swimming pool, cocktail lounge, and restaurant. The rooms were spacious, bright, and well-appointed, and it was competitively priced—if damned expensive can also be a modifier along with competitive. The grounds and courtyards throughout the complex were landscaped beautifully, had fountains and outdoor fireplaces, and encouraged outdoor time in a safe and secure environment. It looked like resort living at its best.

What can you tell by meeting the staff? They looked the part, and they said everything you would expect them to say. Their care was topnotch, their food was excellent, their activities were the best, and their staff was the best-trained caregivers in the city. They only hired the best and retained them because they paid top dollar, had great benefits, and treated them well. I was impressed but skeptical, based on my experience. Remember, my first impressions for in-home care were positive as well. Still, this seemed like the way to go, so we agreed to work toward having Dana move to Villa.

This is where the too good to be true fairy visits. Don't take this personally. Every facility will show you its best face because they want your business, but do not be so impressed by the furniture and facilities that you lose sight of the most important piece of the puzzle, which is the quality of the care.

The demand for good nursing homes, especially those that have memory care facilities, far outstrips supply. Villa, like the other ones at the top, had a waiting list. I put our name on the waiting list and started planning and waiting for the move. I would introduce Dana to the idea and take her to see Villa after we were notified of availability and closer to the time of an actual move.

Several weeks later the Villa called informing me there was an apartment available for Dana. I went to see the space. It was very nice. It had a great view of the mountains and looked over a beautifully manicured courtyard. I liked it and hoped Dana would too, if she cared at all. I was convinced that I had found the very best Scottsdale had to offer. That was the least I could do for her. Still, it didn't ease my conscience or erase my guilt.

The moving day was chosen, and I started planning *another* move. I selected furniture from the house that would fit her new home and that I thought Dana would like. A mover was contacted, and I tried to get Dawn to come for a visit on moving day. She was uncharacteristically unavailable, but our two dear friends of many years, Carolyn and Bill Patterson, came from Kansas City for help and support—what an unselfish, spectacular display of friendship! I can never thank them enough and will never forget their generosity.

The day before the move I took Dana to Villa for an introductory visit. She was willing enough to go for a ride. On the way I told her that we were going to look at a place we might consider moving to. That went easily enough. By this time in the progression of her disease, she either abdicated to my decision making, didn't care what we were doing, or just plain didn't understand; however, she assumed we were doing it together.

The visit went well. Dana was confused and bewildered but otherwise pleasant. The key members of the staff greeted her and made a fuss over her. We looked at the common areas and then at the apartment that would soon become her home. She thought the place was beautiful, and Villa put on a good show. I'll never know if she comprehended what was about to transpire, or if she understood and thought she and I were just moving to a new place to live. While we were there, the Patterson's were busy organizing and helping coordinate the move on the home front.

I don't know if time compresses or expands in the Alzheimer's brain, but the visit to Villa was a distant memory—if any memory at all. I guess there just wasn't any hook in Dana's brain to catch it as it was passing through. Doctors tell me that there is no pattern as to what or when an Alzheimer's patient may remember something or how long it will be retained, if at all. Some things are hooked, and some are not. Some hooks hold, and some don't; however, progressively fewer things are retained and for a shorter time.

Throughout the day I tried to broach the subject of moving to a new home. Dana just wandered around the fringes of the conversation. Even when I told her that "we" were moving the next day, she seemed only mildly interested or aware. But indeed, she was moving the next day. Ironically, she was moving on February 14. Happy Valentine's Day, sweetheart!

The movers came, and the Patterson's and I did the best we could to keep things going while taking care of Dana and Boomer. You can only imagine—no, you truly can't imagine. It was awful. They moved the furniture and big items. Carolyn and I moved Dana's clothes and personal items in several shifts and trips later in the day and evening. Dana was mystified about what was going on. We kept trying to reassure her. Trying to feed her, keep her calm, watch after her, keep her out of the way—it was more than a handful. I thought the last ten or twenty worst days of my life were the worst, but they didn't even come close. This experience was up near the appendectomy. On top of the move, I was still faced with telling Dana that she was staying in the new home, and I was not.

We arranged her clothes and personal items, made her bed, had dinner with her in Villa's dining room, took her to the apartment with a member of the staff, and told her goodnight. I'll never forget the look on her face. Of all the things she no longer tracked or understood, she seemed to understand this: she was staying, and I was going. She cried. I think she understood. I'll never know. I cried. I had betrayed her. She was angry. She was furious. I had broken the heart of the woman I loved. I was utterly devastated.

I went home. Two hours later I was in the emergency room at the Mayo Clinic Hospital, where I spent the night. The doctors suspected the stress of this particular decision and move had short-circuited my systems. Several tests, some calming medications, and a good night's sleep prepared me to go home the next day.

On the advice of everyone who cared for Dana and me, I stayed away from Villa for several days. I was apprehensive when I went for my first visit with Dana. When I arrived, she was sitting in the living room doing an activity with a dozen or so of the other residents. The activity schedule was one of the deciding factors that led me to choose Villa; I wanted Dana to be active.

At home, all she ever did was sit at the kitchen island and occasionally walk Boomer under my supervision or watchful eye. At Villa, she was with other people in similar circumstances, and they all participated in the activities as best they could and with varying degrees of success. Their activities started right after breakfast and went all day up to and including a movie at 6:30 in the evening followed by bedtime. The next day started again with activities right after breakfast. It turns out the activities were instrumental in getting Dana adjusted and finally accepting her new home. She made friends, and she and her friends loved their activities—all the way from "This Day in History" to making pottery.

I walked into the living room and caught Dana's eye. It was a strange and surreal moment. I couldn't tell what was on her mind if anything. My thoughts were confused as well. I went over and kissed her on the cheek and asked how she was.

She responded, "How would you be if you were left here to die?"

My heart sank. I felt sick.

After an awkward moment, the staff asked me to join the activity. I sat next to Dana and the activity resumed. Shortly everyone, including Dana, was engaged; she had already forgotten that she had been angry—if indeed she had been angry. As that activity wound up, Dana was cheerful and talkative. Then it was time for the next activity. Not wanting to wear out my welcome or overdo, I told Dana to join the next activity, that I had to take care of Boomer and would be back the next day to see her. She pleasantly agreed that Boomer needed attention. We each said goodbye. I kissed her on the cheek, and the parting was uneventful. I waved as I walked out the door. She waved back like nothing was out of the ordinary.

While it still would have some bumps in the road, the transfer had been accomplished. I say transfer instead of move because I saw it as a transfer of caregiving duties, not responsibilities. I was then, am now, and always will be responsible for Dana's goodwill and care. I would come to learn that I had not really transferred the caregiving duties as I thought I had. At a minimum I retained the supervision of duties.

I let my mind open, trying to imagine what it was going to be like living without Dana. On the one hand we would not be living together, and I would miss her dearly; on the other hand we would not be living together, and I would be freed from the constant bombardment of caring for an Alzheimer's victim and the continuous need for supervision. That I would not miss. In reality, I had started missing Dana long ago. Her disease had taken her from me years before the move into a nursing home.

A person with Alzheimer's disease dies twice. The brain withers and retreats, slowly taking with it spirit and personality and a brilliant spark of life; however, the body follows a different schedule, one that is unique to every sufferer. If you love someone with Alzheimer's disease, the grief can seem endless, and you don't experience the closure or resolution of a normal death. You mourn every loss of that precious person, almost as a series of deaths, and the loneliness of your own struggle can be overwhelming at times. You will feel guilty, angry, helpless, anxious, and confused. All these reactions are normal and necessary as you try to find your way; the kindest way to navigate the landscape is to be patient and gentle with yourself and everyone around you. There are no quick or easy answers, but there are answers that will be right for you and your unique circumstances.

I hoped that this paradigm shift would free me and allow me to enjoy Dana in her present and deteriorating state. I could visit with her and talk—as best she could—about pleasantries. We could walk and look at birds, which she had always loved, and nature. We could go for an ice cream or out to lunch. I could enjoy the good and let Villa take care of the bad. No more fighting over showers, brushing teeth, taking meds, getting dressed, deciding what to eat, getting lost, getting to bed. Just good times, I hoped.

Chapter 10:
Saddle Up

Early in the experience of a care facility such as Villa, a care plan is developed. The care plan is the roadmap for the resident's care. Care plans are carefully crafted and are living documents giving the staff the instructions for everything the nursing home has agreed to do for the resident to live comfortably, safely, healthfully, and happily in their new home. For Dana, her care plan spanned *everything* from getting up in the morning to going to bed in the evening, including her love of music and musical activities to the glass of wine she might enjoy with dinner. There was nothing left out of her plan, including everything that might trip her trigger and send her over the edge along with what to do to bring her back. As you would expect, the staff assured me they were highly trained professionals in the care of dementia patients, and I need not worry about their ability to care for and look after Dana. This, they said, was not their first rodeo.

The care plan is also a legally-binding business document—a contract. What care the resident needs is scored, giving the facility the amount of effort and resources needed to deliver the level of care agreed to. That level of care is then translated into how much money they will charge. The level of care Dana landed in resulted in a monthly charge of +/-$7,400, not including incidentals such as nail and hair care, premium meals, and medication administration, which if you can believe it, is considered an extra—similar to buying a car and needing to pay extra for the steering wheel.

It is *a lot* of money and a heavy financial burden, even with long-term care insurance. But it's less expensive than good 24/7 live-in help. I will tell anyone who will listen that they need to buy this type of insurance coverage today. Not tomorrow—*today*. In my view, this insurance is more valuable than life insurance. It gives a family the opportunity to have a life in the unfortunate event they have a loved one stricken with Alzheimer's. Without such insurance—or independent wealth—your only choices are to take care of the patient at home or try and get Medicaid after all other financial resources are exhausted.

Additionally, there is a waiting list for Medicaid, and Medicaid facilities are generally substandard when compared with self-pay facilities. If not a nursing home, what will you do if you already have a full-time job? Still, deciding to move Dana to Villa was a major financial decision as well as an extremely emotional personal decision. It was expensive, but I determined that it was the right thing to do. If Villa delivered the level of care to which they agreed in the care plan, I was willing to pay the cost. In my mind, Dana deserved the best, and I arranged for the best I could find.

This was our first encounter with a care plan. Pay close attention. The care plan is a business document. It is vital going forward because you need to understand that the care plan is a component of the legal contract that exists between you and the care facility. It simply states what the staff of the care facility will do (their legal obligation) in return for payment from you (your legal obligation). Make sure the care plan is comprehensive and includes everything that will be done to and for your loved one because you will expect the maximum and they will deliver the minimum, all other things and human nature being equal.

I visited Dana every day for a time until I figured out that I was doing it for me, not for her. Each time I went to see her was much the same. I would find her in an activity, sit with her for a while, and maybe take her for a walk. Occasionally we would get an ice cream, or I took her out for lunch. These were usually not good outings. The experience of trying to order, complaining about the food, the temperature ...was no better than it was when she was living at home. Why would I take her back to the very things that drove me to move her to Villa in the first place?

I soon learned to have lunch with her in Villa's dining room. The dining facilities were open all day long, and we could have ice cream there as well. I had to learn the hard way that these daily visits were not necessary. Dana couldn't remember the last time I was there—whether it was yesterday or last month—or if I had ever been there at all. Also, I couldn't experience the relief I was hoping for if I went to see her every day. Sure, I didn't have to deal with all the upheaval and confrontations, but I was still reminded daily of the immense and overwhelming tragedy in our lives.

After several weeks, I reduced the visits to a couple of times a week. To make up for my guilt, I took fresh flowers for Dana's apartment each time I went. After a time, I learned that she didn't even notice the flowers. It didn't matter. I still took her flowers. It made me feel better.

One of the things that Villa included in their services was billing our two long-term care insurance companies monthly so that we could receive the insurance proceeds. Since I had to pay them in advance and the insurance company paid in arrears, it was important for them to submit the information to the insurance company timely and accurately. Four weeks after the end of Dana's first month at Villa I had not received the insurance proceeds. I called the insurance companies and found out they had not received any paperwork from Villa.

It was time to pay for the next month, and I had not received the money I counted on to help defray the cost of Dana's care. I had paid $15,000 with no reimbursement. A call to Villa's business office resulted in: *Whoops, we forgot.* After I had finished ripping their lips off, they assured me they would send the insurance companies the information that day.

A month later, I was faced with paying another $7,500, and I still hadn't received a penny from the insurance companies. Another phone call to the insurance companies revealed Villa had indeed sent the information the day they said they would, but they didn't send all the information necessary for reimbursement. They had failed to answer four very simple questions—the supplemental information—that the insurance companies required every month. Insurance companies will do whatever they can to reject or delay payment of proceeds; it's part of their DNA.

Another call to the Villa business office and another part of their anatomy ripped later, they promised to rectify the situation immediately. I was now down $22,500 with no reimbursement. It took yet another month for me to start getting insurance proceeds because Villa did—or in their case, didn't do—it again. They put the wrong date on the most recent attempt, dating it with the current date rather than the date of service. I ended up paying $30,000 for Dana's care before I got one cent of insurance proceeds. All Villa had to do was send the bill, answer the four supplemental questions, sign the form, and date it with the correct date. It took them four months to get it right the first time and only after several phone calls, a couple of meetings, and more anguish that I didn't need. Was this a signal?

Was this a signal? Only in the sense that huge black clouds of billowing smoke in a forest usually signal a forest fire. Yes, it's a signal!

A few weeks into Dana's stay at Villa, I started noticing things about her care that I didn't like, but thought it was all part of the adjustment period—both for Dana and the staff. Also, I didn't want to see things I didn't like seeing. I badly wanted for this to be Dana's new home, for her to like it, for me to like it, and for it to be the right place for a long time. I didn't want to overreact. But after several incidents, I'd had enough; it was time to have a visit with the director of assisted living.

On several occasions I noticed that Dana's hair was dirty and clearly had not been washed. I was told that she had refused to shower that day. I explained to them that sometimes she resisted showering at home with me as well, and I had learned to deflect, distract, and/or approach it in a different way to get it done. I thought that if I could succeed in getting her to take a shower in similar circumstances that a "professional, professionally-trained, experienced caregiver" should be able to do it as well. Besides, I informed them that there were occasions where I saw her on consecutive days, and she hadn't showered or washed her hair for two or more days in a row. They had no comment because what could they say?

I also referred to the care plan that included assisted showering and shampooing. After several confrontations, the director told me the solution was that Dana needed more assistance in showering, which would change the care score and result in higher charges. Alternatively, but for the same price, they offered increased assistance but with fewer showers. Knowing how difficult it was for me to get Dana into the shower from time to time, I reluctantly agreed on fewer showers—every other day—with increased assistance. I warned the director, however, that my visits were going to be random and I had better not come on a shower day and find Dana unkempt and with greasy hair. I expected to get what we were paying for. I reluctantly agreed to Dana not having daily showers, but was willing to accept this new plan *without exception.* Already we were to be getting less than the agreed upon care plan. The director understood.

Dana's once beautiful complexion started going south. In the Arizona climate her skin was dry and chafed, and her lips were cracked and bleeding. Did the staff not notice these conditions, asked the Big Bad Wolf? She was clearly dehydrated. Were they providing her adequate liquids? Were the moisturizers and lip balms she owned merely bathroom accessories? Why did I have to notice this and bring it to their attention? What is the professional, experienced, trained staff doing? What exactly was I paying them $7,500 a month for?

One day I saw half of Dana's left eyebrow was gone. Shaved off. Appalled, I asked what happened and found out that she became frustrated trying to pluck her eyebrow and had used a razor to trim it. That was the monitoring and safety in the bathroom agreed to in the care plan? Anything that was sharp or had a safety issue was to be kept in a locked cabinet in Dana's bathroom to be accessed and used only under the supervision of a caregiver.

Back to the business basics of the care plan. The monthly fee is being paid, but some basic, important personal care of the patient is being neglected here. Dehydration is potentially medically serious, as is an unsupervised Alzheimer's patient using a razor blade instead of tweezers. The simplest and most obvious aspects of care in daily living are clearly not being handled, and yet the monthly fee is charged without value having been received.

Dana continued to have occasional panic attacks and periods of agitation where she was a behavioral handful, but no more than seasoned, experienced professionals should be trained to handle. I got a panicked call from Villa each time there was an episode, with them suggesting that we change her medications to calm her down or that she had a urinary tract infection (UTI). They blamed almost every unexplained or unexplainable occurrence on an undiagnosed UTI, sending us to the doctor's office for urinalyses that always came back negative.

Do you know how many unexplained, bizarre things are experienced in the care of an Alzheimer's patient? Some just about every day. When I decided on Villa, they touted the comprehensive roles their RNs play in the level of care. I never saw an RN on Villa's staff, and their LPNs called me for everything. Additionally, their LPNs were of the caliber that couldn't find jobs elsewhere, in a healthcare environment where nursing was in great demand, or they would not have been working for Villa where they were being paid below the going rate for LPNs. I had hoped to avoid these things by hiring a nursing home for Dana's care and paying them $7,500 a month.

Comprehensive care for Alzheimer's patients?

Know the difference between a registered nurse and a licensed practical nurse. An RN usually has a bachelor's degree in nursing and is licensed to triage, which means to sort clinical symptoms in order of importance; an LPN has a certificate and is licensed only to relay symptoms from a patient to another caregiver, a physician, or RN, for triage. This means that LPNs cannot under the scope of their license, treat patients; they merely report their findings to someone who can treat. The great majority of nursing homes are staffed by LPNs for reasons of cost. Be aware of the limitations of staff, and be concerned if repeated urinary tract infections or flu-like symptoms are either reported or overlooked.

The director called me one day to inform me Dana needed one of her medications refilled and that she would text me a picture of the bottle. When I received the picture, it was for a medication for someone other than Dana. *What?* That's right, someone else's medication. Was Dana taking someone else's medication, was someone else taking Dana's? What other medications was Dana taking that she should not have been? Was she getting all her medications? Was she getting them on time and in the right dosages? How could they screw up medication management? That was probably their most serious responsibility and simply could never happen.

Those and several other questions came to mind along with several disastrous scenarios that might result from the possible answers to those questions. Of minor interest was that I paid above and beyond the care plan for medication administration. I called the director immediately. I'm sure my concern and rage were evident, but she casually and nonchalantly told me that she would check the drug cart and let me know.

I was at her office door before she had a chance to call me back. Her explanation was that the staff gave her the wrong bottle for the picture she sent and that everything was in order regarding drug administration. I was asked to believe that and to believe it was the only time that kind of *minor* slip-up had happened. I believed her, and I also purchased some swamp ground in Louisiana from her before I left.

One of the things I had looked forward to when moving Dana to Villa was the relief of administering all her medications and turning that burden over to healthcare, medication management professionals—for which I agreed to pay $400 a month above the cost of Dana's care. Clearly, I was going to sleep better at night after this experience. Not!

I have been calm until now, but here is where the gloves come off! Medication errors ARE EXTREMELY SERIOUS. They raise serious concerns about the systems and processes that MUST BE in place to protect the SAFETY OF THE PATIENT. This one thing is the most important task when caring for someone in an assisted care facility or nursing home: RIGHT PATIENT, RIGHT MEDICATION, RIGHT DOSAGE, RIGHT FREQUENCY. One error here means that nothing can be assumed to be done correctly. Pay attention to the mechanics of medication administration. Is there a drug cart? How are individual patient medications kept separate? How are medication administrations charted in the patient's medical record? By whom? Is there a locked cabinet in each patient's room that contains their medications? Who has access to the code or key? How are nursing orders managed? How are verbal orders for changes in dosages documented? You must be absolutely confident about these items.

Dana's laundry was scheduled to be done twice a week. When I visited with her, I noticed that was not always being done. With more important things to worry about regarding her care, I didn't think this was a major deal. It was not a hill I cared to die on. If her laundry was done once or twice a week really didn't bother me, even though I was paying to have it done twice per her care plan.

The commitment made for laundry was that each resident's laundry would be done separately from any other resident's laundry. By segregating every resident's laundry, Villa said they could assure us that no laundry would be lost or misplaced. That sounded eminently reasonable to me. Unfortunately, it didn't work that way. In checking Dana's clothes from time to time to assure myself that she had what she needed when she needed it, I discovered that some of her clothes were missing and some clothes hanging in her closet were not hers. It's curious that this could happen when her clothes allegedly were never commingled with those of any other resident.

I always wanted Dana to look nice. She had always been put together and well dressed. Since she no longer recognized how she looked or no longer cared or didn't know the difference, I knew she would have wanted me to make sure she looked good. I always bought expensive clothes for her and expected them to be kept safe for her to wear. I went overboard for someone in her condition. Four or five outfits for each season would have been enough. A dementia patient can't make choices very easily and the less to choose from, the better. In clothes for an Alzheimer's victim, less is more. That said, I still bought her too many clothes, and I remembered what I had bought. It was easy to see when they were missing.

I complained each time something was missing and returned strangers' clothes when I found them. Each time I was met with wonderment as to how that might have happened because they always did Dana's laundry separately. Every time I complained, the director said that she would *visit with the staff* to make sure they were doing the laundry correctly; and each time I asked she told me the staff reported that their procedures were being followed.

It was a mystery to everyone. It just couldn't be happening, even though clothes were missing, and other residents' clothes were in Dana's closet, and only the staff was taking Dana's laundry out and returning it to her closet. I was expected not to believe my lying eyes. Villa doing Dana's laundry was another burden lifted from my shoulders. Fighting Dana over the laundry and her losing and misplacing clothing was something I knew I wouldn't miss when deciding to move Dana to the nursing home. But now I had to be involved and constantly fight Villa to keep track of her laundry. And I was paying them to do it. Something was very wrong with this picture.

There is an important practical point regarding laundry, aside from the significant inconvenience of misplacing items of clothing. In stating that each resident's laundry would be done separately, the facility was acknowledging an important safety concern. People in assisted living facilities and nursing homes live in close proximity to each other, and this creates a situation in which germs and viruses can easily spread from person to person. Even with meticulous handwashing protocols from the nursing staff, it's difficult to control the spread of infection, especially during cold and flu season. By washing each resident's laundry separately, the possibility of viral transmission and bacterial cross-contamination is reduced. It can never be eliminated. If separate laundry is offered as part of your care plan, insist upon it.

Dana had a favorite perfume. With or without a shower, she would always spray some on. She loved the fragrance, as did I. One day I noticed her perfume bottle was missing. It had been virtually full the last time I saw it, but God only knows how much she might have sprayed on in the interim. I bought her a new bottle and took it to her the next day. That bottle was missing on my next visit. Someone was stealing her perfume. I alerted the director and lodged a complaint. It was expensive perfume, and I would have nothing to do with someone stealing from a helpless Alzheimer's victim—let alone Dana. I got the standard: *I'll visit with the staff about it.* No acceptance of responsibility. It's always someone else. Let's shove responsibility to the lowest level in the organization. I informed the director that the next time it happened, I would subtract the cost of the perfume from the monthly bill before I paid it and intended to do the same thing with missing clothes. Maybe that would encourage them to take responsibility for caregiving run amuck.

I bought another bottle of the same perfume and gave it to Dana on her birthday. Shortly after that, the bottle was missing. I deducted the cost from the monthly bill along with a couple of items of her clothing and paid the reduced amount. They never questioned the amount I paid. It was easier for them to let me pay less than for them to solve their problems. That realization really opened the door for me.

Shortly after the last perfume episode, I took Dana a bottle of relatively inexpensive perfume. Interestingly, and not surprisingly, that perfume remained in her bathroom until she used the entire bottle. It appeared the less expensive perfume didn't hold the same appeal as the designer brand.

This sad episode illustrates a simple truth: Don't have any item of value in a nursing home or assisted living facility.

Wanting to relieve myself of constantly trying to keep track of Dana's things didn't work out too well by moving the responsibility of her care to Villa and paying them to look after her and her things. I still had to worry about and keep track of everything while paying someone else to do so. What a deal.

Throughout this considerable time, when I visited Dana on shower days I would find her showered and shampooed about half the time. Rather than take the issue to the director—only to have her visit with the staff about it again and to no avail—I just started paying for a care level below the one agreed upon for Dana's care.When told that my bill had a past due amount, 1 told the business office why I didn't pay the entire amount billed. On the next statement they would credit the amount I didn't pay without saying another word, and without improving their contracted level of care. It seemed easier for them not to deliver on their service promises and receive less money than to perform up to the agreement and be paid accordingly. Curious business model.

Most, if not all, of us are accustomed to paying our bills in a timely fashion and understand it's essential to the smooth and efficient operation of business enterprises. This is not necessarily the case in nursing homes and assisted care facilities. The reason we have emphasized the contract and the care plan as part of the contract is that you are only legally obligated to pay for services you receive under the terms of any contract. This concept is crucial, and we will continue to encounter it, but keep in mind that you are not legally obligated to pay for services that you have not received.

From the very early months, the Villa business office continued to be incapable of submitting complete, accurate, or on time claims to the insurance companies. My solution was to delay payment to Villa until I received our insurance proceeds from the prior month. I told the executive director that's what I would do, and I received no argument from him. More than half the time my proceeds were delayed, so I paid Villa late; it didn't seem to bother them. What a way to run a business. Either their margins were so obscene that they could afford this practice or they were so stupid that they didn't know the difference. I didn't particularly like either of those options.

My whole approach to the business arrangement I had with Villa changed. I would now be in charge of what they received for the care they delivered, rather than paying them what they charged for whatever care Dana might receive. Hopefully this would help improve Dana's care if they tired of me not paying all our monthly charges. I didn't know if it was their obscene profitability that drove this change in our relationship, or if it was their stupidity. I hoped it was the former, but feared it was the latter.

Don't be shy about speaking up for your rights here. You are always in charge of paying for services received, and for not paying for services that are not received. The essential wording is this: I WILL NOT PAY THE FULL AMOUNT OF THIS BILL BECAUSE YOU ARE IN MATERIAL BREACH OF THE CONTRACT, AND THAT MUST BE RESOLVED. For example, don't pay for items or services that are not properly documented. Keep meticulous records and be prepared to challenge the accuracy of statements you receive. Avoid signing up for automatic payments because it removes any leverage you have to extract payment for performance within the terms of your contract.

When visiting Dana over a period of several weeks, I noticed that she was almost always with two other residents: Joan and Gloria. At first it seemed reasonable and quite harmless. They participated in activities together, had meals together in the dining room, went on sponsored outings together, watched movies together, walked from activity to activity together—escorted, of course—and generally hung out together. It was always in the company of all the other participating residents, but somehow they had clearly formed a clique. The staff told me that Joan and Gloria had adopted Dana as their leader. Dana was considerably younger, fitter, and with her underlying pleasant personality, was an attractive friend for them to have. The staff said that Joan and Gloria would go nowhere or do nothing unless Dana was going or involved. They said Dana had assumed the role of leader and *took care* of her two groupies.

As first it seemed endearing, and I thought it might be meaningful for Dana to have a purpose in her mind. I started to change my opinion as time passed and my awareness of this relationship continued. Dana was spending more and more time with Joan and Gloria, to the exclusion of everyone else. The three of them would sit on a couch together holding hands with Dana in the middle. Joan in particular, and Gloria to a lesser extent, were becoming very possessive of Dana and resisted anyone's attempt to separate them. When I visited with Dana, Joan didn't want me to take Dana from her, and when I suggested to Dana that we go for a walk or something, Joan would grab hold of her arm and try to hold her back.

The staff told me that this possessiveness was becoming increasingly entrenched. Joan was dominating Dana, which was limiting what she could do, where she could go, and who she could socialize with. Unless Joan acquiesced, Dana was otherwise bound to her. I had to start being forceful during my visits to have any time with Dana away from Joan. It was time for me to have a long visit with the staff, particularly the director. This relationship had to stop.

I told the staff that the situation with Joan had become unhealthy for Dana, and they needed to bring it to an end. I explained the troubles, discomfort, and frustration I was having in my increasing confrontations with Joan, and that it wasn't my responsibility to separate them. When I came to visit, I wanted to see Dana socializing with residents other than Joan. And Joan needed to cease physically clinging onto her.

They agreed that it had gone too far and promised to correct the problem. They also told me that Dana was a big help to the staff in that they were able to accomplish more with everyone when Dana was with Joan.

Great. Now Dana had joined the ranks as an unlicensed, unpaid caregiver.

I saw no noticeable change during my ensuing visits. Joan continued to smother Dana. I arrived for a visit one morning and found Dana sitting in the living room on the couch next to Joan with Joan holding onto her arm. There were no caregivers around. When I attempted to have Dana join me, Joan would not let go of her and demanded to know where I was taking her. That was very upsetting to Dana, who was—and always had been—reluctant to hurt anyone's feelings - in this case, Joan's.

Nonetheless, I extracted Dana to take her to a pottery activity she usually attended. But on that day she didn't go because Joan didn't want her to. Joan followed us all the way, harassing me and complaining about me taking Dana away. When we arrived at the pottery class, the activity director would not let Joan enter. She told me that Joan was not allowed into pottery because she so disrupted the activity. Interesting. Joan couldn't go to pottery because they couldn't control her, so they used Dana to babysit with her instead. I was furious.

I told the director that this bizarre, unwanted, and unhealthy behavior must stop and must stop *now*. Joan had made Villa a hostile and unhealthy environment for Dana and, unfortunately, Villa let it continue. Dana deserved a place to live that was enjoyable, peaceful, healthy, and stress-free. I also told the director I would no longer tolerate Joan's abrasive eccentricities and unwanted advances; their seasoned, professional, and trained Alzheimer's caregivers better figure out a way to control the situation.

The next time I visited Villa, the residents were doing an activity in the living room. Joan was sitting next to Dana holding on to her arm. I turned around and walked into the director's office. She was in a meeting. I canceled her meeting. I told her that I had been patient to a fault and that my patience had just run out. I demanded they provide Dana a living environment without the unwanted, intrusive, and unhealthy exposure to Joan. I wanted Dana freed from Joan's bondage, to enjoy her home, and to participate in all the activities she so enjoyed. Dana was not the problem, yet she was made to feel uncomfortable because of Joan's intrusive, unseemly, inappropriate, and unhealthy behavior.

I told the director to tell the executive director that I wanted Joan's hands off Dana and that I wanted that result *today*. My next stop, I suggested, would be to the State Board of Health. I concluded with a question and a statement. The question was whether or not their crack, experienced, professional caregivers knew how to manage and care for dementia patients—which she did not answer. The statement was that she should tell her boss that I intended to pay Villa nothing for the current month's stay and care for Dana at Villa. Since this issue had been going on for months, since I had demanded resolution several times and since Dana was Joan's de-facto caregiver, I thought one month free ($7,500) was reasonable compensation. I told her if the ED had any problem with not getting paid, I would be happy to bring my documentation of the care issues to a judge and let them determine. I heard nothing back. The regular bill came at the end of the month. I did not pay it. The next month's bill showed the prior month's amount credited to my account without another word mentioned.

I don't know what happened to Joan. On my next visit she was gone, and I never saw her again. I felt badly. It was a shame that I was forced by Villa to do what I did. Poor Joan. She was a suffering soul, and it wasn't her fault. She didn't know what she was doing. I felt and continue to feel for her. Villa simply was presented with a situation that they had no clue how to handle—and no desire to figure out. Yet those are precisely the kind of things that families of loved ones suffering from Alzheimer's disease ought to expect the professionals in charge to handle seamlessly since they are charging a fortune for Alzheimer's care.

Money is the only leverage anyone has with a nursing home. The episode with Joan is one more clear indication that nursing homes require constant vigilance and intervention by the family caregiver to ensure the facility and staff do what they say they will do and have agreed to do. Just moving Dana into an assisted living facility did not provide the relief I expected. You get some relief by having alone time and not fighting the battles and Alzheimer's obstacles 24/7/365, but you remain continually engaged in policing the nursing home.

As I pointed out earlier, meal planning, preparation, executing, and consuming results in several daily flash points in the tumultuous care of an Alzheimer's victim. Carrying in or eating out eliminated some of those flash points, but did nothing to relieve the overall stress and confrontations arising at mealtime with Dana. It was a significant area I hoped to achieve some relief from by Dana's move to a memory assisted living facility. The move accomplished the desired effect surrounding the nuts and bolts of getting Dana fed. There were other unexpected issues that arose, however. I learned now that I had to worry more about the things that I didn't know would happen as well as the things that I did know and was trying to avoid. I got rid of some of the problems but inherited a fresh batch of new ones.

Villa's dining facilities were first rate. The assisted living dining room was beautiful. It provided for either indoor or outdoor dining (nice to have in the Southwest desert) and was beautifully appointed. The kitchen was shared with Villa's restaurant and cocktail lounge for independent residents and guests. Dana had the best of both worlds. She could eat from the assisted living menu which was included in the monthly fee and gave the residents a choice of about four entrees with an array of accompanying items for each meal. If she didn't like what was on that menu, she could choose to order from the extensive restaurant menu for an upcharge.

I thought this was a great deal in the beginning. As it turned out, these options were the worst possible presentations to put in front of an Alzheimer's patient for several reasons. Any well-run nursing home should know that offering numerous choices to patients with dementia is always a disaster. Remember, less is more.

What was I thinking? Dana had not been able to manage meal choices for a long time even with my help, so there was no way she could manage choices with very little or no help from the dining staff. They should have known to limit dining choices to Alzheimer's sufferers. You should just serve them their meal, and make it a well-balanced, tasty, nutritional meal. Remember, they could eat the same thing at every meal and not know the difference. They can't remember the last bite, let alone what they had for dinner last night. Four choices on the assisted living menu were too many. The addition of a restaurant menu to choose from was insane.

Dana learned early on that the restaurant menu had a couple of items on it that she liked: filet mignon and cheeseburgers. From that point forward she completely rejected the assisted living menu and ordered filet mignon and baked potato for dinner, and cheeseburgers and French fries at lunch. While she couldn't navigate a menu or make choices without help, she somehow could remember cheeseburger at lunch and filet at dinner. It was cute at the beginning. I thought this was a phase that would pass, but it didn't. First, it was costing us about $300 a month in up-charges, and second, she started gaining weight. Over the course of about six months, Dana gained thirty pounds. She went from a size 8 to a size 14. Can you imagine the set of opportunities this created for me trying to keep her in clothes that fit?

The longer I cared for Dana, the more I realized that she didn't need many clothes. Four or five outfits for each season; thankfully, there were only two seasons in Scottsdale - nice weather and hot weather. It was still a problem as her size was changing every few weeks. I learned to buy clothes that were comfortable, had some stretch in them, and had elastic waistbands. It was still an expensive headache for me and a bothersome burden.

What was more important, however, was Dana's health. Her weight gain was not good, and her doctors and I agreed her caloric intake had to be curtailed. I tried everything with the staff. They simply had no clue how to execute the doctors' (and my) orders. We told them to stop serving her steak and baked potato for dinner and cheeseburgers and French fries for lunch. I kept getting bills for those meals. Their explanation was that Dana refused to eat anything else and insisted on the steak and hamburgers. We told them to suggest salads. They failed. We told them to tell her the items she wanted were not available. They failed. We told them to serve half portions. They failed. They were told to practice deflection, distraction, and lying, as any seasoned caregiver should know. They failed. On top of this, as with most things in a nursing home, the staff looked for an easy way out. Rather than work with her on menu selections and work through solutions to confrontations, the wait staff would often simply ask Dana if she wanted *the usual.* Simply put, the "professionals" had no clue how to control Dana's diet or the environment around her.

During the time we were searching for diet solutions, the Joan thing was going on. She insisted on sitting next to Dana at every meal, would confuse Dana by what she was eating, and would suggest inappropriate things for Dana to eat. She would make a scene when someone tried to intervene and help Dana because in her mind Dana belonged to her, and she wasn't willing to share her with anyone.

The nursing home's nutrition regimen was totally lacking. Their management of patients was totally lacking. It was up to me to try and figure it out. At one point they suggested I hire a support assistant to help Dana with her meals. They went on to suggest the assistant could help her get up and shower in the morning, arrange and keep track of her clothes, help her in activities, and get her from activity to activity—I wondered what they thought we were paying $7,500 a month for.

I'll never recover from the large piece of my mind I gave them, and they may never sit again from the large piece of their ass they lost from my tongue lashing. Their reasoning was that they would have to devote more time to Dana to satisfy my demands, and that would result in a higher care score, leading them to charge us more each month for her care. I never wavered for a second nor did my position ever change. I told them that until they could execute even their most basic care duties in our contract—showering, hair washing, clothes washing, proper meals—that I would not tolerate an increase in charges. As it was, I seldom paid them what they had been charging anyway.

The meal battle was never solved at Villa, although through working continually with the kitchen staff, slight improvements were made from time to time. While Dana didn't lose any weight, my constant attention to the matter resulted in her not gaining any more. We achieved a holding pattern, with very little help from the Villa staff.

On the administrative side of the dining experience, our bill had erroneous charges on it most months. Dana would be charged for meals she had not received, or she would be charged for multiple meals at one sitting. I would review the bill for dining charges every month and pay what I thought looked reasonable. It didn't bother Villa. They just wrote off what I didn't pay. What do the poor souls do who don't have someone fighting for them day in and day out? Poor Aunt Maude doesn't stand a chance.

So, while no longer preparing meals for Dana and helping her order when going out, I still was engaged in everything she ate, when she ate it, and how she ate it. The pattern became increasingly clear. The nursing home fails on even the most basic elements of care, and the caregiver continues to be more engaged than should be the case considering the promises made by the institutions and the money charged by them.

The valuable lesson learned is that in reality the resident, or resident's family, oversees the relationship if care is not being delivered as contractually agreed. The leverage is money. Don't pay them! There is very little chance they either can or would try to evict the patient. They will avoid the legal issues and having their name in the media for substandard care at any cost. Keep contemporaneous and meticulous records of all issues, communications, and conversations. It's my experience that nursing homes aren't managed well enough to document the issues, and they are unlikely to want to document instances where they fail miserably in delivering the level of care that any reasonable person should be able to expect. Even though they told me that this wasn't their first rodeo, it had become clear they had no idea which end of the horse was the front.

These examples of Villa's monumental failure to deliver even the basics of care promised are only a few of the dozens of issues I had to deal with. I was disappointed with Villa and was becoming disenchanted with nursing homes in general. I couldn't get a break from Dana's care. Every time Dana had any issue, no matter how small, I received a call from the staff wondering what they should do. Their staff was low paid, poorly trained, inexperienced, and unfit for the job they were obligated to do—the same thing I got from in-home caregivers.

When I was caring for Dana at home, the task became overwhelming. I came to realize that watching after her in a nursing home was still a full-time job and more than I bargained for, considering I was paying a premiere nursing home to care for her. I didn't know what to do next. Villa had to work. They were the best in Scottsdale. I couldn't bring Dana back home. I visited with folks who had loved ones in other highly regarded institutions and heard the same horror stories. Moving Dana to another facility was out of the question.

What was I going to do?

I had to do something to remedy what we were experiencing— poor hygiene practices, laundry and clothes problems, hostile unhealthy living environment, theft, medication management problems, nutrition and eating issues, activities issues. These and other problems were not sequential. They were all happening concurrently. I felt I had to be involved every day to help Dana, protect her, feed her, and see that she was safe, secure, and being taken care of. The level of care promised during the sales cycle and the level of care contracted for and spelled out in the care plan simply was not being delivered.

Just when I was at my lowest and questioning my decision to move Dana to a memory care assisted living facility, Dr. Anne Kenworthy, God bless her, came to my rescue again. Looking back, I'm convinced that she is an angel sent from heaven. I know now that I would not be here today had it not been for her professional judgment, great friendship, and guiding hand. I can only hope, dear reader, that you experience a relationship with your personal physician that is similar to mine with Dr. Kenworthy.

As you might expect from a Mayo Clinic physician, she has superb expertise and an outstanding reputation as an educator, researcher, and clinician. In person she is disarmingly warm and unfailingly kind, with a quick smile and a calming presence. She is tall and graceful and moves with swiftness and confidence without ever giving the impression of being hurried. The overriding impression of time spent in her examination room is that you are the only patient she has ever had. Her focus is utterly fixed on the concerns you bring to her, and despite her formidable medical knowledge she engages her patients in a conversation as she offers information to help guide the decisions that you make together about your care. She is tender in times of pain and unflinching in her devotion to my best interest as her patient.

Dr. Kenworthy knew of a former Mayo Clinic nurse who had started a sole proprietor nurse advocate business. Dr. Kenworthy told me that I should call Gretchen, tell her about my experiences with Villa, and see if I wanted to hire her to intervene with Villa on behalf of Dana's care. She was not the assistant Villa had suggested

I hire—someone to do their work. She would be someone to monitor what they did and give me assurance they were doing their job and doing it right. She would take me out of the line of fire and be my first line of defense from the monster nursing home. Additionally, she would be my first line of offense. I struggled with the idea of needing to hire and pay someone to be a quality control mechanism for the nursing home. Nonetheless, I called Gretchen.

Chapter 11:
Call to the Bullpen

Five years post diagnosis...

I loved Gretchen the minute I met her. She and I bonded immediately. I had enough experience at this point to recognize excellence. Gretchen had all the qualifications I expected from someone Dr. Kenworthy recommended, but at our first meeting I realized that Gretchen's character was as much a qualification as her extensive nursing background. She had an outstanding reputation as a clinical nurse, but her absolutely unflappable, charming demeanor and meticulous attention to spoken and written detail were encouraging indicators to me that she would be an effective advocate for Dana's care.

Moreover, Gretchen had a soft, lovely sense of humor and a commonsense approach to life. On first impression and in every subsequent meeting, I had the feeling of continuing a conversation with a friend as well as a superb nurse, and I fervently hoped that Gretchen would bond with Dana in the same way she and I had bonded. As I said earlier, the challenge with nursing patient advocates is that the good ones are busy and have too much to do already. The others you don't want to hire. Miraculously, Gretchen made space in her practice for us, and I had no doubt that she was one of the good ones.

She could insert herself into the mix and check on Dana, and Villa, three or four times a week. She understood the problem; she had done this before. Clearly, this was not *her* first rodeo. She convinced me that she could provide me with the relief I so desperately wanted. After seven or eight years of fighting Alzheimer's from the outside, I'd had it. Gretchen was expensive. I don't know what people who can't afford it do. Either their loved one suffers the failures of the system, or the caregivers kill themselves trying to get quality care for their loved ones. The result is the same as if the nursing homes hadn't come into the picture and the loved ones stayed home. What an indictment of the system we have when someone has to hire a personal RN advocate to protect the rights and dignity of the nursing home victim.

While things didn't turn around overnight, hiring Gretchen was a home run. By that I don't mean that Villa might turn around or improve. Theirs is a flawed business model that will take a complete revamping to improve. I mean that Gretchen gave me immediate relief. Not total relief, but measurable relief in a short period of time.

I gave Gretchen a medical power of attorney for Dana's healthcare and informed Villa that when she spoke, she spoke for me. They were to take any order she gave them as though it came from me. They were to report directly to her anything that required reporting regarding Dana, and they were to report it to her before they reported to me. She would triage whatever came to me. She was to protect me and use me only when necessary in the management of the relationship with Villa. I was as much her patient as was Dana. Quite simply, I told Villa that Gretchen was in charge. Now all I had to do was convince myself that was the case and try to step back a little.

Gretchen was a machine. She hit the ground running. In no time, she was monitoring Dana's shower and hair washing schedule and riding Villa to adhere to it. She made sure they were treating her complexion and that they were assisting Dana in dressing properly. Now she wore matching outfits and clean clothes. Gretchen arranged her closet so that it was organized and easy to keep outfits together. She inventoried all Dana's clothes, marked every item with a permanent marker and set up a spreadsheet to keep track of everything. She saw to it that the laundry was done on schedule, returned to her room, and put away properly. Soon the missing clothes became less of an issue. Funny how you can begin to expect what you inspect.

Dana would often bring leftovers from her meal to the apartment and put it in her little refrigerator. As you might imagine, she would immediately forget it. Her only activity with her refrigerator was to put things in; she never took anything out. Candy and edibles that I would take to her would also go into the refrigerator. Housekeeping never cleaned out the refrigerator, even though they had been told to do so on several occasions. After a while all the things in her refrigerator were either green or brown. Gretchen would routinely clean out the refrigerator and soon even got the housekeeping staff to occasionally take a look, actually doing part of the job they were getting paid for.

Gretchen set up a routine where she monitored Dana's medications and Villa's medication management. What a crime that nursing homes can't be trusted to execute even the most basic, yet most important, responsibilities and duties. She monitored Dana's vital signs and weight, kept meticulous records of everything, and forced Villa to do the same. She would compare records randomly to make sure Villa continued to do their job.

Villa had a responsibility to take vitals weekly, yet when Gretchen came on the scene and checked, there was no record of that ever having been done. Villa told Gretchen that they did check vitals and weighed her weekly, but had not recorded the findings because they were always within norms—like they would know what normal was. They went on to sell Gretchen a bridge in New York as well. After

Gretchen's arrival, Dana's records were complete and up to date. I can only imagine how incomplete the other residents' records were and continue to be.

Checking Dana's weight weekly, we could now start monitoring the success of the attempts to improve Dana's diet. Gretchen worked with the kitchen staff, the wait staff, and the caregivers to continually work on healthier eating habits. She forced Villa to make sure that Dana—and by association, the other residents—was properly hydrated during the day. Until Gretchen made a big fuss of it, residents would only be given something to drink when they asked for it. Think about it. When would an Alzheimer's victim think about asking for a drink of water? They don't recognize when they are thirsty. Gretchen made Villa staff understand how to dress Dana properly. Outfits didn't always match as we would have liked, but it reduced the times that Dana was found dressed in a blouse with her pajama bottoms.

Gretchen was a great help assisting Dana and coaching the staff through the activity schedule for the memory impaired. At the beginning, I thought the activities as described would be great for Dana. Certainly they would be better than sitting at the kitchen island at home all day. They were described as keeping the resident occupied and engaged without being overwhelmed. They were to be geared to accommodate severely reduced cognitive abilities and included everything from lunch outings, museum visits, and an occasional baseball game to simple, daily thought and motor activities.

In reality, the activity program was totally out of sync with the condition of the residents. The activities were not carefully chosen or thought out and were executed by untrained, inexperienced, and unmotivated staff. The typical activity leader was the next minimum wage employee hired by Villa to replace the one that had just left. They were place-keepers, someone to sit in the room with all the folks struggling through various levels of dementia. They had no experience and received no training whatsoever in dealing with Alzheimer's patients.

Gretchen went on lunch outings and watched the struggles of ordering from menus. She saw Dana demanding a cheeseburger and fries in a Chinese restaurant. They would choose exotic and trendy restaurants and present the fares to folks who would be happier with a grilled cheese and bowl of tomato soup; however, the activity director was happy. The activities seemed to satisfy the people running them. Thinking about the participants didn't seem to be a priority. I guess those choices made Villa think they were creatively contributing to the struggling participants.

Other activities were boring, uninspired, and inappropriate. For example, they had a daily "This Day in History" session. Imagine a discussion of what happened on this day in history with a room full of people who couldn't remember if they had eaten breakfast, taken a shower, brushed their teeth, or tell you the name of their children, the state they lived in, what day it was, what year it was, or what happened five minutes ago. Mind you, they were a group of patients suffering different levels of memory loss. Some could remember better than others. Some who couldn't tell you what day it was or if they had breakfast could recall events that happened years ago. Often, but not always, short-term memory fails sooner than long-term memory fades. Having them all in the same activities is totally inappropriate, counterproductive, and frustrating to the participants. In many instances it's cruel seeing them suffer through the exercise. And an activity that works for someone today very well may not work tomorrow. Get the point?

Simply, the activities were filler. They put a minimum-wage person in with a group of Alzheimer's patients to keep an eye on them while they charged a premium rate as a leading-edge memory care facility. When Gretchen or I sat in on an activity, half of the attendees were asleep, and the rest were staring off into space.

We challenged the management of Villa to improve their activities program by pointing out the issues we saw. When pressed, they agreed that the program could use some *tweaking*. Criticizing the program resulted in the activities director punishing us, and by association Dana, by ignoring her and otherwise excluding her from things she might have enjoyed. This treatment was obvious to both Gretchen and me and got worse as time progressed.

It finally sent me over the top.

The despicable reaction on the activities director's part was met with more hostility from me than she bargained for. I demanded a meeting with the executive director, the assisted living director, Gretchen, and me. I got the meeting when and where I wanted it. I told them what they could do with their activities director if we observed this kind of behavior to any extent at any time. If either Gretchen or I saw even a hint of her treating Dana in any way but absolutely perfectly, the next voices they heard would be from my lawyer and the licensing agencies of the state of Arizona. I concluded by asking them if they had any doubt about what I had said. They said I had made myself perfectly clear. I followed up the meeting with an email to all attendees documenting the discussion in detail.

Activities can be helpful, but sometimes they create unexpected complications. Activities must be suitable to the psychological and physical condition of the participants, and they should be flexible to allow for changes in patients' abilities. If the enjoyment disappears, the value also disappears. Pay attention to the dynamics of the group, especially with regard to exclusion or unhealthy behaviors such as bullying.

Even in a nursing home, Dana would get sick occasionally. She would get a cold, the flu (both respiratory and intestinal)—all the usual things that everyone gets. Alzheimer's doesn't help avoid other illnesses, it amplifies and complicates them. I expected to be called every time Dana fell ill and was. These episodes have been infrequent, but when they come, they are particularly difficult and stressful. The Alzheimer's victim doesn't do well when they get sick. They don't understand, they get very confused, their symptoms are magnified, and they simply can't follow any directions in dealing with or treating their ailments. Taking care of them is frantic and stressful. I hated getting those calls, but that was part of the ongoing responsibility no matter where Dana lived or how much care she received. Luckily for me, Dr. Kenworthy was always at the end of the phone and would see Dana when necessary, which she did. After Gretchen arrived, she often handled the crisis with minimum intervention from me. Gretchen would hold Dana's head when appropriate, and Dana seemed to do better with Nurse Gretchen than with me anyway.

Some of the worst days in the life of Alzheimer's families are holidays, which no longer meant anything to Dana. She had stopped experiencing the anticipation of holidays long ago and didn't understand or participate in the celebration with any acknowledgment. On the positive side, Alzheimer's has spared her the post-holiday depression we all feel. As most caregivers probably do, I continued to try to make holidays special for Dana. She was always a great holiday celebrator. Her love of life and great generosity lifted everyone's spirits at holiday time, and she loved the holidays. I tried to do as much as I could to continue making those days special for her, until I realized that everything I did, I was doing for me, not for Dana. Once the Alzheimer's victim reaches their individual tipping point, nothing means anything to them, and most things that are done for them are for the benefit of the doer. I guess out of sympathy, compassion, love, or guilt.

Holidays were/are much worse with Dana in a nursing home than they were at home, particularly when I had to leave her at the end of a holiday visit. Gretchen helped buffer the downside of holidays by her cheery and uplifting presence. Suffice it to say that holidays are not positive, memorable events in the lives of Alzheimer's patients and their families.

Once Dana moved to the nursing home, she never came home again, and I made no attempt to bring her home. Home was never mentioned again, and she never seemed to notice. The doctors and I concluded that taking her home could only serve to disrupt her new life. If she noticed, it might cause anxiety or confusion at best. Home to an Alzheimer's patient is where they happen to be at any point in time.

Gretchen was a lifesaver, indeed. She helped transform Dana's new home. I continued to be engaged as I knew I always would be, but Gretchen's presence greatly diminished the level of my engagement. We were finally experiencing assisted living—hygiene, dressing, eating, health, socializing, proper medication, guided activities. The only problem was that it was Gretchen and me who were managing most of the assisting. I'll never know or understand what the institutional nursing home considers the elements of assisted living to be and for which they charge. Actually, they know; they just don't care.

All the care experiences up to this point crystallized in my mind that my involvement in Dana's care would never end. Of course, I have always known that my responsibility for her care, comfort, and well-being will never end. It wasn't my intention to disengage myself from her care. After doing it alone for as long as I was able, my subsequent decisions were to relieve me as much as possible, so I could last as long as possible. Also, my decision process was affected by my financial resources.

All decisions made by caregivers will be influenced by the resources each has, both personal and financial. They will make different choices at different times, and those choices will vary; however, they all have the same problems faced in common.

Chapter 12:
Time Out

Six years post diagnosis...

To reduce the wear and tear on me, I was always willing to commit as much money to Dana's care as we could afford for as long as we could afford it. Even so, I always tried to keep the expense commensurate with the services we received. At first I tried the part-time, in-home model for two reasons: First, to see how Dana (and I, for that matter) would react to having someone other than me helping her. Second, I was trying to save as much money as possible. The support in this model didn't work, and whatever it cost was not worth the money. Plus, I was still *fully* engaged in this model.

Next, I tried the full-time, in-home model with Sherri. As you saw, this model worked for a time but ultimately failed because I couldn't find the best to hire. Also, with Dana still in the house, I was partially engaged during the day and on duty full-time every night and weekends. This model was expensive, and the cost would have been prohibitive to have 24/7/365 coverage with really good staff even if they could be found. An additional downside would have been losing my privacy.

Unfortunately, the corporate, institutional model fails the care-giver as well. I was relieved most days from the turmoil and direct care but was continually affected by the institution's substandard service and lack of caring. It's better than 24/7 in home care and less expensive, but you're kidding yourself if you think it will relieve all the pressure.

With a nurse advocate the expense goes up, but the pressure goes down accordingly. The amount of involvement by the nurse advocate is a cost/benefit decision assuming you have a good one, as was our case. The more they are involved, the better your quality of life. At this point in the stage of Dana's disease and care, it was the best option for me, and I prayed every night that nothing would happen to Gretchen, and I wouldn't run out of money.

After all the fits, starts, and grief, I finally began to settle down and started to build a new life. Gretchen and I were a good team, and Villa, for all its faults, was as good a home as we were going to find for Dana as long as we were vigilant and willing to leverage non-payment for their failures.

Gretchen and I got into a routine with Villa and each other. Gretchen coordinated Dana's care with my input and visited Villa four or five times a week. I visited Dana a couple of times a week. Gretchen and I spoke a couple of times a week by phone and met for coffee a couple of times a month. I was about as comfortable with Dana's care as I could be and was somewhat satisfied with my ability to have a life outside of Dana's care. My mind was clearer than it had been in years, and I felt more optimistic than I had since being hit by Dana's diagnosis. We had a plan and were executing it. Gretchen did her part marvelously, I did my part, and Villa did some of their part or didn't get paid. Now, Dana's care was *only* a full-time job.

Throughout these care experiences, Dana's personality went from vibrant to blank, her health from vital to frail, and her cognitive abilities from relatively bright and alive to helpless and hopeless. Her memory faded slowly at first but then more quickly until it became an Etch-a-Sketch, where there was nothing in advance of the dot and very little evidence of anything trailing the dot.

Life started to settle down for me, and a pattern developed where I had time to work on a future for me while still engaged to a lesser extent with Villa and Gretchen in Dana's care. As the weeks went by I became increasingly comfortable and optimistic with how life was proceeding.

Then one day out of the blue, Dana's daughter, Melissa, called and asked if I would consider moving Dana back to Kansas City to be closer to her and her family—Melissa's spouse and Dana's two darling granddaughters. The request came as a surprise; up to that point she had shown relatively little interest in Dana's condition or care. Dana also has two sons who live in nearby mid-Missouri. Dana loved her children and adored her granddaughters. As it happened, she was not particularly close to her children, but in normal circumstances would have loved to be near her grandbabies.

When we left Kansas City, we did so after careful consideration. Dana wanted to live in the southwestern desert. She loved Scottsdale, as did I. Another attraction was the Mayo Clinic; we thought Dana had the best chance of extending a reasonable existence under its care. We knew we were leaving our friends and Dana's daughter and family behind. We would miss our friends, but the distant relationship Dana had with her family had given her no reason to believe that she would miss them—except for the little girls. Besides, at that point we still were residents of Kansas, and we thought we could return for visits or have the granddaughters visit us. We hadn't fully realized the impact of the death sentence Dana received. We promised to stay in touch with friends and hoped to add to the few friends we had made in Scottsdale over the years. As it turned out, thoughts of relationships fade early in an Alzheimer's patient as their mind turns inward. I missed our friends, but everyone faded from Dana's memory because of her disease.

Don't assume you need to seek care at a sophisticated medical center; just be sure that the medical help you have is right for you and your individual needs and circumstances. Seek out people who take an interest in you and who show you through numerous ways that they care about your loved one.

Melissa's suggestion was intriguing. I was sure that family would be a great comfort to a caregiver, and I would welcome all the support and help that family was willing to give. To this point, the only family support and assistance I received in Dana's care came from my daughter, Dawn, who made as many trips from Denver as she was able to. Dawn loved Dana as though she were her own mother. That and her spirit to always help her dad when she could was all the motivation she needed. Whatever the motive, I welcomed all the many that times Dawn pitched in. The result of Dawn's devotion was that she was among the very last to fade from Dana's mind. The memory of and the love for Dawn remained in Dana's mind long after she had forgotten her entire family, except for Nurse Bonnie.

I was also skeptical of Melissa's overture because of her previous lack of any meaningful engagement in Dana's care, but I would welcome Melissa taking a lead role. If I moved her to Kansas City, I knew I might miss her greatly. But then again, I already missed her and had been missing her for some time. The Dana I knew, the light of my life, was gone and had been gone for a long time. I realized that missing her any more than I already did was not possible. A change in her body's physical location might benefit me and would do nothing to change her.

In fact, there were good reasons to move Dana. Her granddaughters could grow from the experience of knowing their Nana even in her diminished condition. Their presence might brighten Dana's life, although that would be an unknown to everyone except for the far reaches of whatever Dana's mind could process. Additionally, whereas Gretchen and I were Dana's only real visitors in Scottsdale, Dana's many friends in Kansas City could—and I knew would—drop in to see her from time to time, thereby hopefully bringing a little more light into the darkness of her existence. And I could fly to Kansas City to visit often and check on her care and well-being.

I believed it might be the best solution for both Dana and me. It's sad to say, but moving her would have a more profound effect on my future that it would on hers. Whatever her motives, I'm sure Melissa was not doing this for my benefit. Had benefiting me been a consideration, I would never have received the call.

After several conversations, Melissa convinced me that she and her family were committed to taking the point position in her mother's care, and I agreed to move Dana with the knowledge that wherever she resided, the final responsibility for her care was and always would be mine.

I coached Melissa over the next few months on finding an appropriate nursing home for Dana. Leaving Villa wasn't going to break my heart, and we very well might find something better. At that point in my experience, I was still cautiously optimistic that there might be a good institutional, corporate nursing home out there. To her everlasting credit, Melissa executed her due diligence admirably, narrowing the choices to two possibilities that I interviewed. Not surprisingly, both said the same things and promised the highest level of care as did Villa. They were newish, shiny, beautiful facilities. They had *the best staff money could buy, the staff was experienced and well trained, the activities for the residents were stimulating and appropriate, medication management was top drawer, the environment was safe and healthy* ...a second chance to get completely out of debt. And, of course, they both had waiting lists.

The icing on the cake, the *coup de grace,* so to speak, relating to Villa occurred ten months after Dana moved out. Sitting at home on a hot, sunny afternoon in the desert, my telephone rang. It was a collection agency saying that our unpaid account for $10,460 with Villa had been turned over to them for collection. Mind you, there had been *no* communication whatsoever with Villa for ten months, I had received no correspondence from them of any nature, and it is illegal to initiate a collection action against someone without any notification.

I guess you might say that I went ballistic.

The temperature in the desert was nothing compared with how hot the blood was that was rather forcefully pumping through my body. I telephoned Villa's executive director and was relieved that he was in and took the call. I might have exploded had I not been able to reach him. There was no way that this was going to be a civil discussion. I can only paraphrase what was said. I'm not going to write the words that were said, nor the tone in which they were expressed.

I informed him of the phone call from the collection agency. He responded that he knew absolutely nothing about it and would have to check into it.

Clearly, it was time for me to buy some more Louisiana swamp acreage from him.

I told him that there had been absolutely no contact in any form from Villa since Dana moved. I had no idea what the obscene dollar amount they were trying to extract from me represented. I had received no bills suggesting that anything went unpaid after Dana's move, and I had their final statement after her move that showed our account was paid in full. I demanded that he immediately send me any documentation that supported the unpaid account.

I then told Villa's executive director that I believed they had broken the law by placing my account with a collection agency without ever communicating with me, and if it proved damaging to my credit rating, it would expose them to civil litigation I would be all too happy to initiate. By then he was aware I would welcome exposing our experiences with their patient care to a judge. And finally, I demanded they retrieve our account from the collector.

He listened, which was all I wanted him to do. I was determined to do all the talking. He said he would check into the matter. I encouraged him to do so.

The next day I received an email from the executive director saying he was making progress on the matter and would have an answer and the documentation the following day. The next morning I received a phone call from him. In the softest, gentlest tone you can imagine he told me to forget about the call from the collection agency, my account had been retrieved from them, they had made a big mistake, we owed them nothing (zero, nada, nil), and he was sending me a statement indicating such. When I pressed him to send me the detailed information they had sent to the collection agency, he stammered, stuttered, and would only reiterate they had made a terrible mistake.

I did receive a statement with a zero balance to add to the one I already had. Later, I also received a letter of apology from Villa's corporate management, which I had demanded. I also had them document there would be no evidence of the collection action on my credit report since it was falsely initiated. Where the $10,000+ came from and how it got on our account and how our account got to a collector remains a mystery to Villa, as does how to deliver quality care to Alzheimer's patients.

Chapter 13:
Déjà Vu All Over Again

Seven years post diagnosis...

We chose a new home for Dana. Another move, 1,500 miles away! It could not have been done without Gretchen; however, we did it without Dawn needing to take another rescue trip to Arizona. It was a monumental undertaking with an Alzheimer's patient. Getting Dana's things packed and moving them along with her furniture was one thing, moving Dana was entirely another. Driving for two days would have been a disaster and flying commercial not much better. The answer was to fly private, and our dear friends, Chuck and Jennifer Laue, offered their G-2000 to get Dana to Kansas City.

Arrangements were made and executed. Gretchen accompanied her and told me the flight went very well, even though Dana had no clue what was happening. She and Dana had lunch and a glass of wine on the plane, and they sang most of the way. Melissa's family met Dana and Gretchen at the airport in Kansas City, and with as little pain as possible, Dana arrived at her new home in Leawood-Sunset Village (Sunset). I don't know if Dana understood that she would not see Gretchen any longer, but I would surely miss her. When she came in from the bullpen, she struck out the side. What a great closer.

The beginning of life for Dana at Sunset was not dissimilar from her start at Villa. Their sales staff said the same things we had heard at Villa. After long discussions with them about my prior experience with Villa, I was assured their administrative staff was well versed and efficient at billing and dealing with long-term care insurance carriers, and their bills were audited for accuracy before they were sent. I hoped they would and could deliver, unlike Villa. More importantly, our most fervent hope was that Sunset would actually provide high-quality, consistent, compassionate care for Dana in a safe and comfortable environment. All that was left was to develop and agree on a care plan for Dana.

By now I was well versed in putting together a care plan, so this was a familiar drill. The plan was better and more complete than the first plan at Villa. My prior experience helped make it more complete, and it was made crystal clear what Sunset's commitment was to Dana's care. Every detail was included of what they would do for Dana, from getting up in the morning to going to bed at night. It included hygiene, safety, laundry and cleaning, diet, activities, medication management, health management and any special needs or requests.

Experience had taught me that it would take some time for the staff to adjust to Dana and for Dana to adjust to her new environment, although I'm not sure Dana even recognized the change. She had demonstrated long ago that her memory of yesterday was nonexistent. She wouldn't have known if she was in Kansas or Arizona, and she wouldn't have cared. I'm not sure whether that included her environment or the people around her. I didn't expect instant success across all fronts. I only hoped Sunset would be an improvement from the experience we had at Villa and they would deliver the care they agreed to in Dana's care plan. Since I was in Scottsdale, I had to rely on Dana's daughter to take the lead in monitoring Dana's care, which she agreed to do. I told her what to look for and how to respond if things weren't going as expected or didn't look right.

Melissa and I communicated by phone, email, and text over the next few weeks. She reported that some things weren't getting done to her satisfaction, but it seemed that progress was being made. She said everyone was pleasant to her and seemed to be nice and considerate toward Dana; however, early on she voiced concern over continuity of staff. We had been told and assured in the sales cycle that Dana would have specifically-assigned care staff. That was their commitment so her caregivers could become familiar with her needs, her moods, and her eccentricities. We agreed that seeing the same people all the time would be comforting and less confusing and upsetting to Dana, and that consistency and continuity would be better than someone new all the time. The same caregiver(s) would become "friends" with Dana. Seemed like a great step forward in caregiving compared with what we had at Villa.

Unfortunately, delivering continuity of care was not happening. Melissa reported that each time she went to visit with her mother, she met someone different who was working on getting Dana through the day. When this pattern continued, Melissa asked the assisted living director about their policy of caregiver continuity. This concept was news to the director. When I was told that residents received assistance from whoever happened to be wandering by when assistance was required or requested, I called Sunset's executive director and asked for clarification.

He told me that the idea of consistent caregiver contact was something they would aspire to accomplish, but that it didn't always work. When I told him that during the sales cycle we had been assured we could expect it most of the time, he said they would "do the best they could" to make it happen. Well, it didn't happen, and neither Melissa on her frequent visits nor I on my occasional visits ever once saw the same caregiver. What is it with these people, promising you one level of care—and charging you for it—then delivering a lower level of care and expecting you to agree with it? I was disappointed, but by now not surprised. I expressed my displeasure to the executive director who seemed to shrug it off.

Some time had passed before I made my first visit to Sunset to see Dana. I made the visit about a couple of months after she moved in. I arrived late morning, checked in at the front desk, introduced myself, and asked where I could find Dana. The receptionist was a teenager and appeared perplexed by the question. Not knowing who Dana was, she looked at what appeared to be a resident register. She informed me that Dana was in her room and gave me directions to it on the second floor.

I went up to the second floor via a wide open, beautiful winding staircase, wondering why the design of the facility would include such a hazard considering the residents' many physical and mental challenges—and propensity to wander around if not watched. I filed that thought away for a later date. I found Dana's room and went in. No one was there, so I went back downstairs and inquired if anyone knew where I might find Dana. No one shed any light on her whereabouts and suggested that I might look around to try and find her.

A little curious, you might think?

I started to wander through the facility. In a short while, I located Dana in the dining room alone. I mean *alone*. There were no caregivers, no dining staff, no maintenance people, no one. She was sitting in a corner staring off into space dressed in her pajamas. She clearly had not showered. The condition of her hair suggested it had not been shampooed for several days. Her teeth weren't brushed. She had no idea where she was, couldn't tell me how she got there, if she had eaten breakfast, or if she had seen anyone around anywhere at any time. She looked absolutely pitiful and sad. I was furious.

SERIOUSLY?? After all this time, after all the lessons learned, we are again confronted with the INEXCUSABLE! Unscheduled, unannounced visits can be extremely helpful in revealing the events of everyday living when you are not around. You can assume that what you see on a random visit is what happens ALL THE TIME unless they can prove otherwise. THIS IS NEGLECT. THIS IS POTENTIALLY NEGLIGENT, AND YOU SHOULD NEVER TOLERATE THIS.

I located the assisted living director and demanded some answers. I wanted to know how it could happen that I found Dana in this condition and warned her not to tell me that this was the first time something like this had happened, knowing full well it was highly unlikely for such a failure to happen for the first time when I made a random, unannounced visit. She made no excuses. More troubling, she offered absolutely no explanation as to how an Alzheimer's resident could be abandoned and found in this condition with no one on the staff knowing where she was.

Clearly, no one had bothered to check on Dana this morning or assist her in getting ready for the day, or get her to breakfast, or get her to an activity, or engage her in any way. After I had extracted my pound of flesh for this episode, the director told me that they do the best they can. I later came to find out that was code for: *This is all you're going to get.* At Villa it was: *I will visit with the staff.* At Sunset it was: *We are doing the best we can.* My question was, is it the best you *can* do or merely the best you *will* do?

After discussing the circumstances and condition I found her mother in with Melissa, she told me that she too had noticed that her mother wasn't getting showered and shampooed consistently, wasn't getting dressed timely or very well (unmatched or dirty clothes), and that she often found her sitting alone. And where was the world-class activities schedule?

It was time for a meeting with the executive director to tell him I wasn't going to do all the things I had agreed to—namely, pay them the agreed charges—since they were not doing everything they had agreed to and were contractually bound to do. We scheduled a meeting on my next visit. In the meantime, I pointed out that Dana's care plan included shower and shampoo every day, assistance with other hygiene necessities like brushing teeth, moisturizing skin, etc., assistance with dressing in clothes that came close to matching, assisting with getting Dana to meals, and including Dana in activities.

A couple of months later—now four or five months into Dana's stay at Sunset—I met with the executive director and Sunset's senior staff. They used the meeting to inform me the care we expected for Dana would require them to charge more than originally agreed, not to address their failures, which was the reason the meeting was scheduled. It was *déjà vu* all over again, and corporate nursing home standard practice—promise what the patient will get and how your loved one will be cared for then don't do what was promised and agreed to. And when you are called on it, demand to be paid more than originally agreed and deliver less than originally promised.

The nursing home took the position that Dana required more care than they originally estimated, even though their Alzheimer's *trained, expert caregivers* agreed to the original care plan. I took the position that until they were able to demonstrate that they could execute and deliver the minimum, basic level of care any expectation for increased charges on their part would be dealt with by my delete key. I had seen this outrageous nonsense before.

Their insistence that the problem was Dana and they were doing the best they could do really lit my fire. This meeting, several follow-up telephone calls, and future face-to-face meetings confirmed that with all of Villa's faults and failings, it looked like a five-star resort compared with Sunset.

When I insisted they were not providing even the minimum level of care one should reasonably expect, like getting a shower and getting hair shampooed every day, they initially insisted that it was getting done. When I proved to them that was not the case, they said that it was always done unless Dana objected to getting a shower. Where had I heard this before? Villa, that's right. I explained how to deflect and redirect if Dana resisted, which was something their *expert, experienced, highly regarded staff* should know.

At one point, I agreed to shower and shampoo three times a week as a counter to their insistence for higher charges because of shower fatigue. They agreed that the showers would be given on Monday, Wednesday, and Saturday. Dana had her hair shampooed and styled on Thursdays by the beauty shop in Sunset. That would give her clean hair four times a week and keep her body relatively clean the entire week. Trying to be flexible and get along, I reluctantly gave up four showers a week to keep the monthly care charges the same.

At the end of the month, it was clear by Melissa's visits that Dana was not getting even the agreed to three showers a week. When we pressed the issue, sometimes they would tell us that Dana's shower was skipped on the day scheduled and given the next day, adding: *What difference does it make?* I'll tell you what difference it makes. They have a care plan they are obligated to execute, and the care plan spells out what will be done and when.

How about medications? The care plan dictates what medications are to be administered and when. If Dana resists taking her medications, do they just skip giving them or give them at unscheduled times?

Do they pick and choose which elements of the care plan are followed and which are not? How are we to have any confidence that anything in the plan is being done as agreed? The care plan is carefully constructed with the family. It is the contract between family and institution regarding the care of the patient. It isn't to be completed and filed away to satisfy some agency and not referred to when caring for the resident. Every caregiver I asked about Dana's care plan told me they had not seen it. They told me they only do what their supervisor tells them to do. Clearly, the supervisors either didn't know what was in the care plan or didn't care. It turned into a war of words where they said they were, and we said they weren't. We had carefully documented days when Dana had not been showered. Obviously, they were only on days when Melissa or I visited, so there were many days we couldn't prove. Again, it is reasonable to conclude that the only days that Sunset failed weren't just the days when we visited.

Since they told us in the beginning that their crack caregivers kept daily care notes, I asked for copies of the daily care notes for September 13 through October 28. I thought this would either support their position or confirm my suspicions. When they sent the notes, many were missing: September 20, 24, 25, 27, 29, October 2 through 14, October 18, 19, 22, 23, 24, 25, 26, and 27. When pressed, they did not respond to my request for the missing notes that they steadfastly said were meticulously maintained daily. Case closed on the shower issue. I paid them half of the next month's charges and never heard a whisper from them. The next invoice showed no previous balance and the account paid in full. Apparently they went to the same school of management as Villa.

The mid-September through October period covered by the request for their daily notes proved to be a watershed time for our relationship with Sunset. Dana's prescription glasses—her vision was considerably impaired without them—were lost during this period. They assured me that the caregiver always made sure her glasses were on when she got up in the morning and were taken off when she went to bed. I know she wouldn't move in the morning without them, and she never took them off. They were missing for nine days before Melissa found her without them on a visit. No one at Sunset either noticed or cared that she was stumbling around without them, nor did anyone inform either Melissa or me about her missing glasses. Remember, she can't see very well without her glasses, and she was wandering around Sunset's second floor where there was the big, winding open staircase leading down to the first floor.

I told the staff that the glasses had to be in her room. They needed to search the room thoroughly, and I told them how to search inch by inch. They said they had combed every inch. Even the executive director said he had personally looked at every inch of the room.

Melissa took her mother to get an eye exam and bought a new pair of glasses. Several days later, the glasses were found by Sunset's crack caregiving staff in her room under the chair next to her bed. I don't know how long they had been lost before Melissa noticed, but housekeeping thoroughly cleaned every room twice a week per their sales brochures, and the entire staff including the executive director searched every inch of Dana's room for her glasses multiple times. Not!

On the subject of their meticulous housekeeping, one day Melissa went to visit her mother in the early afternoon. She found her in an activity in relatively good spirits. After the activity, she wanted to take Dana out for some ice cream. With Dana waiting for her downstairs, Melissa went to Dana's room to get her coat and found feces all over the floor in Dana's bathroom. It was caked on and in a state that suggested it had been there at least since early morning or possibly even the day before. Since Dana had not returned to her room—nor could she without being accompanied—and since she left it after getting up and ready for the day, what does this shocking condition say about the quality of the caregiving?

Dana also got the flu during this eye-opening time period, and no one cared to inform either Melissa or me. The family absolutely must be informed when their loved one falls ill. There was no excuse for not notifying us, and they offered none; however, they said their nurse had seen Dana and that everything was under control.

Another serious event. The failure to communicate an illness— even a mild illness, such as a cold—to the family is a breach of the contract of care. You have every right to know if your loved one is feeling unwell or is not eating normally or reports unusual symptoms to the nursing staff. Be sure to ask to see the nursing notes on one of your unscheduled visits. The notes should be readily available and provide reassurance that your loved one's health is being carefully monitored and documented. Make sure the notes are current. Anything less is unacceptable.

As it turned out, Sunset had no RN as they led us to believe when we made the decision to move Dana there. They had a couple of as-low-as-you-can-pay-and-can't-find-work-elsewhere LPNs. I have nothing against LPNs. There are good ones and bad ones just like every other profession. The good ones don't work in places that pay as low as large corporate nursing homes. When I found out all they had were LPNs, they explained they had a community RN who came to see every resident every month, checked how they looked, answered any questions the LPNs might have, and took and recorded the residents' vital signs.

Since Dana had been ill with the flu, I was interested in the course of her illness and subsequent recovery. They should have had their own LPNs' notes and records and the community nurse's monthly notes and vital sign information. I asked Sunset to send a copy of those records to me for my review. They couldn't seem to locate any of these records on Dana. Wow. I became so furious that I referred to our contract with Sunset where there were provisions for escalating complaints and grievances. Since the only responses I received from Sunset's staff and management was either no response or *We are doing the best we can*, I grew tired of their abysmal performance and decided to go to a higher level.

The escalating process went from the facility's executive director, which I had done until I was blue in the face, to Sunset's district director, their regional director, then to their corporate office, and finally to the State Department of Health. I decided to skip the district director and start with the regional director. I called the number listed and got voicemail. I left a message stating the reason for my call and leaving a call-back number. Two days later, having received no return call, I placed another call and left a similar message on voicemail. Three days after the second call elicited no response, I repeated the exercise.

After two more days, I called the executive director at Sunset and told him I was escalating my issues. I told him that his boss's boss was not returning my calls and that my next call was to the State Department of Health.

Guess what? The regional director returned my call within the hour. She apologized and told me that she seldom checked the voicemail for the telephone number published in their complaint escalation procedures. Seriously?

In addition to the issues I outlined, there were other items of note I covered in my conversation with Sunset's regional director. The activities calendar was not always followed; scheduled activities were often canceled for no apparent reason. Evening activities were particularly susceptible to cancellation. When activities were canceled, it left Dana with nothing to do, and Sunset had no alternate plan for residents. Dana would just sadly sit alone until someone came by to take her to her room and help her into bed.

On one visit I found her sitting alone waiting for her hair appointment. Everyone else had gone on a fun off-campus outing, but she had to stay behind for her hair appointment. The only problem was it wasn't her hair appointment day. Accordingly, she missed a fun outing and didn't have her hair done. She just sadly sat alone for the day. That was yet another example of their cluelessness regarding the schedule or whereabouts of their residents.

We also discussed their continual attempts to increase charges above the agreed amount. The care-plan-charge-increase caper was the most obvious, but medication management ran a close second. Before we moved in, we furnished Dana's prescription medication list to Sunset at their request so that they could determine their charges for medication management. Within the first month, I was told that Dana's medication management charges were going to be increased because of the number of medications she was taking, which had not changed from the list we originally provided. Nonetheless, they said after further review they were going to charge more.

I told them, and reiterated to the regional manager in our conversation, that I didn't care how much they charged me. I said that I was going to pay them what we had originally agreed, and I didn't care what they did with the unpaid balance. I was tired of the bait and switch, referred to our written agreement, and said I would welcome a discussion with a judge regarding their billing practices. They never tried to collect the higher charge, and I never paid it.

Speaking of billing, Sunset was no different and no better than Villa in submitting monthly billing information to our long-term care insurance companies. I didn't stress over this one because of my previous experience at Villa. I merely told them, and reminded the regional manager, that I would pay my bill—or whatever part I thought was appropriate considering their poor care practices—when I received our insurance proceeds. They could choose how soon they wanted their money by how efficiently and accurately they cared to be in providing the insurance companies the information required to pay benefits. As was my now acquired practice, I seldom paid our bill in full as they seldom delivered the level of care and service they were contractually obligated to deliver, and what I did pay, I seldom paid on time because of their inability to bill accurately and timely.

I informed the regional manager that I intended to move Dana at our earliest opportunity. Chapter and verse, I pointed out how dismal their care of Alzheimer's patients was. It was worse than dismal; it was disgusting, depressing, and dangerous. Nothing I said seemed to bother them. They couldn't care less if you moved out and didn't pay. They were in an indefensible position and would not even try to collect.

You do not need to tolerate indefensible behavior. You cannot make an institution care if they are inadequately staffed or managed incompetently, but you do have the strength of your moral principles and the protections of your legal contract. Don't be shy about asserting your rights to protect the well-being of your loved one.

They were happy to see the patient with advocacy leave. They would just call the next victim on their waiting list and hope that sucker didn't have someone looking out for them very carefully. It's no wonder that the average stay in a nursing home is three-and-a-half years. I'm honestly surprised anyone lives that long. I was left with no reasonable alternative. For Dana's health, welfare, and safety, and for my peace of mind, I had to find a new home for Dana that understood caring for people living with Alzheimer's. Yes, Sunset was *déjà vu* in every respect, but they gave us some "vuja de" as well—stuff we had never seen before and wished we had not experienced.

The cautionary tale of our experiences is this: As desperate as you and your family may feel in your need for emotional relief and the reassurance that someone is constantly watching over the Alzheimer's patient who is so much a part of your hearts and lives, you cannot ever remove your focus or relax completely. I'm sorry if that hurts or disappoints you, but the sad fact is no corporate model of care can hope to equal the care that is given so freely from the heart. My hope is that your journey, though different from mine, will bring you to a place of peace, knowing that you have done the best you possibly could.

We tolerated the next several months in anticipation of hopefully finding a better solution for Dana's care.

Chapter14:
Home on the Range

Eight years post diagnosis...

As another support institution failed the Alzheimer's victim and caregivers, the search began to find a new home for Dana. The only thing I knew for sure was that her next home would not be the large corporate model. I didn't think I was asking for too much. All I wanted was a quality, compassionate, safe, healthy, and secure home for Dana that truly understood Alzheimer's disease and what it took to care for its victims—not just lip service.

I wanted a place that would work with me to develop a care plan that made Dana comfortable and kept her as healthy and safe as possible and did it consistently. I hoped to find a place that would contact me with any issues, keep me informed about any changes or problems, and answer their phone when I called. Also, it would be nice if they could help me with insurance claims on a timely basis.

I didn't and don't expect perfection. I expect them to try their best to do what we agree is in Dana's best interest and make an honest effort to improve when they fall short. I'm willing to work with someone who is willing to work with me and for Dana. I want commitment, compassion, and caring. For my part, I will gladly pay them the agreed upon price. In short, I wanted a place that said the right things, did what they said, and charged for what they did. Pretty simple if you ask me.

I was anxious to let the sun set on Sunset and get Dana to a place that would be better for both of us.

After considerable reflection on my experiences and considerable research on available alternatives, Melissa and I found a place that showed promise. I interviewed them extensively, checked their references, and carefully looked at their facilities. The owner understood my issues and offered common sense, understanding, and compassionate solutions. He was aware of and sensitive to the problems I had encountered at corporate nursing homes. He had seen it and experienced it, and he was determined to offer alternative solutions to their failures. He was passionate about his model and personally participated in its execution.

Jerry, the owner and founder, had spent his career in the funeral, hospice, and healthcare fields. He had visited hundreds of senior living locations and found most to be less than ideal. When his own grandmother developed dementia, she was moved several times between nursing homes, skilled care facilities, and hospitals. That experience inspired him to develop a better, more personal dementia care that large institutions either did not, would not, or could not offer. His facilities were called SeniorCare Homes, and they offered neighborhood living for the memory impaired. Jerry transformed residential houses into secure, safe environments that look and feel like home yet offer specialized care for folks dealing with Alzheimer's disease.

Each SeniorCare home cares for five to eight people at a time to ensure each resident receives personalized attention on a daily basis from licensed caregivers. It's very much like living at home. While they offer scheduled activities, many of the residents' activities are helping in the home with usual domestic chores. This environment promotes self-esteem and peace of mind for the residents, preventing the depression of being in an isolated room or being left alone somewhere in a large facility. Also, the caregiver is never far away, so supervision and care are just steps away, and the residents are always under a watchful eye.

On the practical side, they provided everything one would normally expect in their own home. Dana would have her own room and bathroom. They would help her with all daily living tasks including bathing, dressing, grooming, and personal hygiene. Medication management is a given. The residents got delicious home-cooked meals, which they could even help prepare if they were willing and able. Snacks and beverages were available anytime. The services included laundry and housekeeping, in-house entertainment, outdoor walks and activities in a beautifully landscaped yard with walking paths, and anything else a resident may have a particular interest in.

The caregiver and the residents functioned very much like a family. Moreover, this total-care philosophy, combined with the resident's care plan, came with a set monthly fee and no hidden costs or add-ons. The charge included everything they promised to deliver.

Novel idea!

Jerry understood that when it comes to memory loss, living in the moment is everything to the stricken. In addition to the individualized care, SeniorCare creates spontaneous moments of joy, which gives purpose and meaning to each day.

They also have true continuity of care. Allowing for work schedules, the same caregivers are with the residents every day. They get to know them and bond with them as a family would. I liken the caregiver to a housemother looking after the needs of those under her care.

While very skeptical because of my prior experiences, I felt that moving Dana to SeniorCare was the next right decision in the painful journey of caring for her. They had the usual waiting list all memory assisted facilities have—both good and bad. We spent our time on the waiting list until an opening in one of SeniorCare's homes became available, and we moved Dana to her next new home.

She has now been at SeniorCare going on two years without me having one thing to criticize them for. They have performed as promised. They have done what they said they would do, including processing insurance payments timely and accurately, when they said they would do it. And I have paid them for their great care for Dana. They have a real RN, as promised, who gets to know the patients and their eccentricities, and she treats them with care and compassion.

I receive a call to inform me of any issue with Dana. The call is to inform me and assure me that she is being taken care of, not to ask me what they should do. She has fallen ill from time to time, has panic episodes, slips and falls, periods of combativeness—stuff happens. I'm kept informed as necessary as the SeniorCare staff handles the issues in consultation with Dana's doctor. As needed we discuss all elements of her care. Dana still doesn't like to take showers, but miraculously they find ways to get her through the process. Even though her appetite is failing, they get her to eat when otherwise she might not, and they always make sure she is nourished and hydrated. Medicines are properly administered, and they work directly with Dana's doctor on any prescription drug issue.

Jerry checks each of his residences and residents weekly. I have a direct line of communication with him and real contact with the caregivers and the entire staff as needed. Dana is clean and dressed in appropriate outfits every day. Her skin is soft and hydrated, her hair is clean and combed, one of the caregivers paints her nails, and she is made to feel loved and cared for. Even though she is totally unaware of her surroundings, I'm aware and thankful that she is in the hands of real, experienced, trained, competent, caring, and compassionate caregivers.

They have proved that a memory care facility can do the right thing. I pray that it continues and have every reason to believe that it will. The nursing home/memory facility conclusion is that there are very few good options, but there are a few. SeniorCare Homes is one of them.

I visit Dana often enough to assure myself that she is well cared for, comfortable, and safe. I make sure that she has nice, soft clothes; that her bed and bathroom linens are nice and soft; that she has safe and comfortable shoes to wear; and that any and all supplies she needs are available. These visits are for me and for the promise I made to her. Even though she is unaware of her surroundings and my visits, I hope somewhere, somehow, they bring her some comfort.

The good news is that hopefully Dana is home. The bad/sad news is that she has no awareness of where she is or what the conditions are wherever she may be. Dana, while still having a smile on her face or humming a song, no longer recognizes anyone, including me. She appears to enjoy seeing me but has no clue who I am. She no longer even recognizes herself when looking in a mirror. The reflection could be anyone but often seems to be someone she likes. She carries on a conversation with whoever she thinks she is seeing at the time but usually asks who that person might be. Often she appears to be trying to have a conversation with an imaginary person.

She has lost her appetite and all the weight she gained while at Villa—and more. She has no interest in food, seems to have forgotten the use of silverware at the table, and often seems not to recognize what food is. Her brain no longer tells her that she is hungry. She is often ill-tempered and combative. She is incontinent, unsteady, and frail. Her Etch-a-Sketch is frozen in time and space with nothing either ahead of or trailing the dot and no hope the dot will ever move again. But she still smiles and hums a melody.

Dana is gone. I miss her and will always remember her as she was.

Afterthought

I have chronicled our Alzheimer's journey through several years. It began with Dana exhibiting unusual behavior and me observing it. It took us to and through doctors' offices, medical facilities, and hospitals ultimately resulting in Dana's diagnosis. We experienced the anguish of a deteriorating brain as we struggled through life trying to find help for Dana's suffering and relief in my caring for her.

Sadly, I know how this story will end for Dana. No one can be sure when it will end or where it will end, but we know that Alzheimer's will relentlessly continue to attack her brain until it finally decides to shut down completely. It will forget how to walk and how to talk or maybe how to swallow or how to breathe, ultimately telling the body it can do no more, having endured all the torture it could bear.

Until that time comes, I will continue to look after Dana wherever her body may reside and pray that her final sleep will be peaceful, blessed by God, and come with a song in her heart. As for me, I'm doing well and building a new life outside and around caregiving. After we sold our home and left our condo in Kansas, I got a place to live in Denver and moved my legal residence from Kansas back home to Colorado where my daughter, Dawn, and her husband, Mark—as well as my son, Greg, and his wife, Lael—live and where I own property. However, I will always keep a second home in the Valley of the Sun.

I will also always be vigilant and responsible for Dana and see that she is carefully and compassionately cared for until the end or as long as I draw a breath. While the light of my life has dimmed, the warmth of the memories will always be with me. Because of those who supported me and looked after me, I can continue to monitor and manage Dana's care without killing myself 24/7/365. I am now convinced that if it weren't for Dr. Anne Kenworthy and my partner Ruth Ingall, I would no longer be here to continue in that manner. They saved my life.

I hope this journey is meaningful and useful to those who have followed us through it, and I hope it provides strength and wisdom to anyone unfortunate enough to find themselves in similar circumstances. As I said in the beginning, the unknowable is what Dana felt or experienced. I'll never know what she knew or when she knew it. There was never a time during these many years when it seemed that she fully comprehended the death sentence she was handed.

Maybe that's the case with early onset Alzheimer's. While you are scrambling to find out what's going on and what might be wrong, the speed of the decline takes the victim past the time they can understand the consequences of their plight. When it seemed that she still had some understanding, the depth of my conversations with Dana seldom went beyond her struggles with forgetting things or the inability to do things she once could. The conversations were matter-of-fact, then emotional, and soon forgotten. Looking back, I'm not sure the conversations were even meaningful when we were engaged in them. I'll never know if she understood and just refused to believe it, if she understood and bravely cast the shadows aside, or if she flat out had no idea what was happening to her. I hope it was the latter. I can't imagine the pain and anguish she would have endured had she truly understood. Thankfully, she is now beyond and far removed from any tortured thought.

I hope.

PS: Dana left us, softly and gently, on February 18, 2018, four years and four days after leaving home. Heaven's choir gained a lead soprano that day...

APPENDIX

Mini-Mental State Examination (MMSE)

Patient's Name: _____   Date: _____

Instructions: **Ask the questions in the order listed. Score one point for each correct response within each question or activity.**

Maximum Score	Patient's Score	Questions
5		"What is the year? Season? Date? Day of the week? Month?"
5		"Where are we now: State? County? Town/city? Hospital? Floor?"
3		The examiner names three unrelated objects clearly and slowly, then asks the patient to name all three of them. The patient's response is used for scoring. The examiner repeats them until patient learns all of them, if possible. Number of trials: _____
5		"I would like you to count backward from 100 by sevens." (93, 86, 79, 72, 65, ...) Stop after five answers. Alternative: "Spell WORLD backwards." (D-L-R-O-W)
3		"Earlier I told you the names of three things. Can you tell me what those were?"
2		Show the patient two simple objects, such as a wristwatch and a pencil, and ask the patient to name them.
1		"Repeat the phrase: 'No ifs, ands, or buts.'"
3		"Take the paper in your right hand, fold it in half, and put it on the floor." (The examiner gives the patient a piece of blank paper.)
1		"Please read this and do what it says." (Written instruction is "Close your eyes.")
1		"Make up and write a sentence about anything." (This sentence must contain a noun and a verb.)
1		"Please copy this picture." (The examiner gives the patient a blank piece of paper and asks him/her to draw the symbol below. All 10 angles must be present and two must intersect.)
30		TOTAL

(Adapted from Rovner & Folstein, 1987)

irce: www.medicine.uiowa.edu/igec/tools/cognitive/MMSE.pdf   Provided by NHCQF, 0106-4

Instructions for administration and scoring of the MMSE

Orientation (10 points):
- Ask for the date. Then specifically ask for parts omitted (e.g., "Can you also tell me what season it is?"). One point for each correct answer.
- Ask in turn, "Can you tell me the name of this hospital (town, county, etc.)?" One point for each correct answer.

Registration (3 points):
- Say the names of three unrelated objects clearly and slowly, allowing approximately one second for each. After you have said all three, ask the patient to repeat them. The number of objects the patient names correctly upon the first repetition determines the score (0-3). If the patient does not repeat all three objects the first time, continue saying the names until the patient is able to repeat all three items, up to six trials. Record the number of trials it takes for the patient to learn the words. If the patient does not eventually learn all three, recall cannot be meaningfully tested.
- After completing this task, tell the patient, "Try to remember the words, as I will ask for them in a little while."

Attention and Calculation (5 points):
- Ask the patient to begin with 100 and count backward by sevens. Stop after five subtractions (93, 86, 79, 72, 65). Score the total number of correct answers.
- If the patient cannot or will not perform the subtraction task, ask the patient to spell the word "world" backwards. The score is the number of letters in correct order (e.g., dlrow=5, dlorw=3).

Recall (3 points):
- Ask the patient if he or she can recall the three words you previously asked him or her to remember. Score the total number of correct answers (0-3).

Language and Praxis (9 points):
- Naming: Show the patient a wrist watch and ask the patient what it is. Repeat with a pencil. Score one point for each correct naming (0-2).
- Repetition: Ask the patient to repeat the sentence after you ("No ifs, ands, or buts."). Allow only one trial. Score 0 or 1.
- 3-Stage Command: Give the patient a piece of blank paper and say, "Take this paper in your right hand, fold it in half, and put it on the floor." Score one point for each part of the command correctly executed.
- Reading: On a blank piece of paper print the sentence, "Close your eyes," in letters large enough for the patient to see clearly. Ask the patient to read the sentence and do what it says. Score one point only if the patient actually closes his or her eyes. This is not a test of memory, so you may prompt the patient to "do what it says" after the patient reads the sentence.
- Writing: Give the patient a blank piece of paper and ask him or her to write a sentence for you. Do not dictate a sentence; it should be written spontaneously. The sentence must contain a subject and a verb and make sense. Correct grammar and punctuation are not necessary.
- Copying: Show the patient the picture of two intersecting pentagons and ask the patient to copy the figure exactly as it is. All ten angles must be present and two must intersect to score one point. Ignore tremor and rotation.

(Folstein, Folstein & McHugh, 1975)

Source: www.medicine.uiowa.edu/igec/tools/cognitive/MMSE.pdf   Provided by NHCQF, 0106-41(

Interpretation of the MMSE

Method	Score	Interpretation
Single Cutoff	<24	Abnormal
Range	<21	Increased odds of dementia
	>25	Decreased odds of dementia
Education	21	Abnormal for 8th grade education
	<23	Abnormal for high school education
	<24	Abnormal for college education
Severity	24-30	No cognitive impairment
	18-23	Mild cognitive impairment
	0-17	Severe cognitive impairment

Sources:
- Crum RM, Anthony JC, Bassett SS, Folstein MF. Population-based norms for the mini-mental state examination by age and educational level. *JAMA.* 1993;269(18):2386-2391.
- Folstein MF, Folstein SE, McHugh PR. "Mini-mental state": a practical method for grading the cognitive state of patients for the clinician. *J Psychiatr Res.* 1975;12:189-198.
- Rovner BW, Folstein MF. Mini-mental state exam in clinical practice. *Hosp Pract.* 1987;22(1A):99, 103, 106, 110.
- Tombaugh TN, McIntyre NJ. The mini-mental state examination: a comprehensive review. *J Am Geriatr Soc.* 1992;40(9):922-935.

Bibliography

"10 Warning Signs of Alzheimer's Disease." *Alzheimer's Association*.
Accessed July 27, 2016. http://www.alz.org/alzheimers_dis-
ease_10_signs_of_alzheimers.asp.

Day, Thomas. "About Nursing Homes." *National Care Planning Council*. www.longtermcarelink.net/eldercare/nursing_home.htm.

Hearing on Fiscal Year 2014 Appropriations for Alzheimer's-related
Activities at the US Department of Health and Human Services
(Statement of Harry Johns, president and CEO of the Alzheimer's
Association.) "Alzheimer's Impact on the American People and
the Economy." *Alzheimer's Association*. Last modified March 13,
2013. http://www.alz.org/documents/national/submitted-tes-
timony-050113.pdf.

Stafford, Diane. "Alzheimer's Care Takes a Toll on the US Workforce." *Kansas City Star*. Last modified February 12, 2013.
www.kansascity.com/news/local/article314571.

Walshe, Kieran. "Regulating US Nursing Homes: Are We Learning
from Experience?" *Health Affairs*20, no. 6, (2001): 128–144.